ARCHAEOLOGY EXPLAINED

ARCHAEOLOGY EXPLAINED

Keith Branigan

Professor of Prehistory & Archaeology
University of Sheffield

Duckworth

Third impression 1998

Gerald Duckworth & Co. Ltd.
61 Frith Street
London W1V 5TA

© 1973, 1988 by Keith Branigan

Distributed in USA by
Focus Information Group
PO Box 369
Newburyport, MA 01950

ISBN 0 7156 2011 8

British Library Cataloguing in Publication Data

Branigan, Keith
　　Archaeology explained.
　　1. Archaeology—Methodology
　　I. Title
　　930.1　　　　CC75

　　ISBN 0-7156-2011-8

Photoset in North Wales by
Derek Doyle & Associates, Mold, Clwyd.
Printed in Great Britain by
Page Bros. (Norwich) Ltd., Norwich.

Contents

To
Vath Sivadith
with our love

Preface

Why are you digging it up? How do you know how old it is? In the space of two decades of work on archaeological excavations I have heard these questions asked by onlookers time and time again. It is for the people who put these questions and seldom get a satisfactory answer that this book is intended. I have written in general terms: not for the 'informed layman', but rather for *all* laymen and students. I hope they will not be the only ones to benefit from it.

'Archaeology *must* win the understanding and approval of the public as a whole, as well as at least a measure of public support. It is my hope that this book will play a small but effective part in achieving this.' When I wrote those words, as a preface to the first version, published in Britain some ten years ago, I hoped that the book would reach a new audience and would recruit new devotees to archaeology. Whether or not it achieved that goal is difficult to judge, but as it passed through a Book Club edition, a paperback version and a Dutch translation, in addition to the original hardback edition, presumably it must have reached a fairly wide audience. As the need to involve the public in support for archaeology has grown rather than diminished since the mid 1970s, I was particularly pleased when my present publisher – for whom I had originally intended the book in 1973 – expressed interest in a new edition. The opportunities to bring the text up to date, to add a new chapter and to extend the range of illustration were all welcome, and I was glad to accept the invitation.

I hope this new edition will reach an even wider audience. In particular I hope it reaches the many thousands of young people who are finding more and more that archaeology provides an exciting and unusual approach to the study of the past, as well as being a fascinating subject in its own right. I look forward to the day when archaeology will have a regular place in school syllabuses, not only in history and classics but in geography, environmental studies and the sciences.

For the illustrations, I am grateful for copyright permission to those acknowledged in the captions. My thanks are also due to Mark Edmonds for drawing, or redrawing, figures 7, 8, 20, 21, 25, 28, 30, 31, 48, 49, 50, 52, 53, 58, 59, 60, 63, 65, 66, and to Gill Stroud for provision of human bone material for photography.

My wife has read the typescript and corrected many errors; she has also tried to ensure that what I have written is both grammatically correct and comprehensible!

K.B.

Illustrations

1. Introduction

Ever since the 1870s, when Heinrich Schliemann uncovered the remains of Troy and in the process revealed a fabulous treasure of gold and silver objects, the achievements of archaeologists have been in the headlines. Schliemann's equally sensational findings at Mycenae, where a rich array of weapons, jewellery and gold masks was unearthed in five shaft-graves, were followed not long after by the discoveries of Sir Arthur Evans at the Minoan palace of Knossos (Fig.1); and while Evans toiled in Crete Hiram Bingham on the other side of the world scaled near-vertical cliffs in Peru to reach the lost city of Machu Picchu, almost certainly the Inca citadel of Vilcabamba. In 1922, before Evans had finished his work at Knossos, Howard Carter discovered the tomb of Tutankhamun. Beside the incredible wealth of precious objects in the four rooms of this Egyptian tomb, the discoveries of Troy, Mycenae and Knossos paled into insignificance. In 1930 the greatest of the royal tombs of Ur in Mesopotamia was excavated by Sir Leonard Woolley, and a few years later came the discovery of the remarkable ship burial at Sutton Hoo in Suffolk. The mid-1950s saw the amazing finds at Jericho, the early 1960s the exotic mysteries of an 8,000-year-old city at Catal Huyuk in Turkey, and the later 1960s the palatial splendours of Zakro in Crete and Fishbourne in Sussex. The decade closed with the discovery of a 'new Pompeii' on the Aegean island of Thera, and the 1970s brought the wealth of written documents of the time of the Patriarchs in the city of Ebla and the richly equipped tomb of Philip of Macedon, father of Alexander the Great.

In the public mind, archaeology is still largely synonymous with the excavation of treasure-filled tombs and lost cities. The glitter of gold has made it difficult for the aims of the archaeologist to be seen in perspective. The layman thinks in terms of material objects and buildings and judges

1. One of the store-rooms of the palace of Knossos, with huge *pithoi* (storage jars) against either wall. Sir Arthur Evans's discoveries, which included a magazine of almost two dozen such rooms, caught the public imagination at the opening of the twentieth century. Photo: K.B.

archaeological skill in these terms alone. But pots and pans, temples and tombs are not what the archaeologist is mainly seeking; they are not the be-all and end-all of his efforts, but simply a means to an end.

What then is the purpose of archaeology?

According to Grahame Clark, it may be simply defined as 'the systematic study of antiquities as a means of reconstructing the past'. Christopher Hawkes gives a fuller definition: 'The purpose of archaeology is to discover, study and interpret the material remains which the prehistorians substitute for written history.'

I hesitate to quarrel with either interpretation, and yet neither is entirely satisfactory. For the archaeologist must concern himself not only with antiquities but with the context in which they existed; moreover there are many archaeologists who are not prehistorians and have no dealings with prehistory. An eminent prehistorian such as Professor Hawkes may be excused for introducing prehistory into his definition, but in this book we are concerned with the widest of archaeological horizons. Glyn Daniel has rightly said that 'archaeology begins yesterday', and with the growth of industrial and post-medieval archaeology this is increasingly true. A journal now exists called *Post-Medieval Archaeology* which, it is hoped, will provide a timely reminder that archaeologists cannot ignore the early modern remains that so often appear in their trenches overlying those of the Roman or prehistoric period. Medieval remains have also aroused less interest than those of earlier periods and, surprisingly, until recently less archaeological evidence existed for the medieval city of Colchester than for its Roman predecessor. The archaeologist often has to excavate a series of levels and associated structures that cover large periods of time and, perhaps, several totally different cultures in various stages of civilisation. While he cannot be expected to have an equal interest in each of these cultures, he should certainly excavate and record every level with equal care and skill. That archaeology is the main source of information for prehistory should not obscure the fact that it can, and does, provide a great deal of knowledge about societies at various historical periods. Any definition of archaeology must take this into account and at the same time try to set out the modern archaeologist's responsibilities. My own definition of archaeology is that it embraces the discovery, recording, preservation (where possible) and interpretation of all traces of man and the world in which he lived before the present.

If this approximates to the modern concept of archaeology, clearly we have advanced considerably from the days when excavations were undertaken principally to unearth ancient artifacts sufficiently sophisticated and complete to be regarded as *objets d'art*. Fortunately the pleasures of archaeology are not confined to such discoveries; if they were, few of the excavations undertaken in Europe and North America would attract the thousands of volunteers who work on them each year. These volunteers come not only because they have a fundamental interest in the past but because they enjoy the task of archaeological detection. It might be said that detection is the aim of the archaeologist, and much of this book is concerned with the ways and means by which he detects and the problems facing him as he does so. It is in the field of detection, of course, that the archaeologist, who is intent on discovering all his clues *in situ*, differs from the plunderer. He will wish to know the associations of everything he finds; discoveries made out of context, unless recognised as such, will completely falsify the evidence from which he will reconstruct his picture. Once artifacts are removed from their original context they are of little archaeological value, because it is the acquisition of knowledge rather than the accumulation of objects that is important. For this reason, if for no other, excavation has become a science in terms of the approach adopted and the techniques employed. The process has often been compared to a laboratory experiment, but there is an essential difference: excavation is by nature destructive and cannot be repeated.

Excavation, however, is only a third of archaeology. There remain the study and the interpretation of the evidence; and, while the study of the evidence is becoming increasingly scientific, the interpretation of it is still much less so. The archaeologist is trying to bring humanity to light from a collection of artifacts, structures and scientific observations. He is therefore inevitably concerned with man's mind and

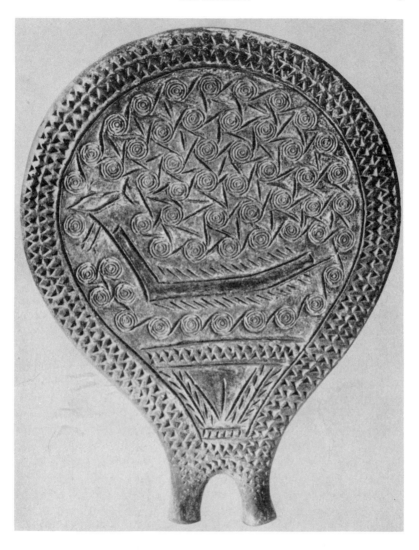

2. A so-called 'frying pan' (*c.* 2500-2000 BC) typical of a large group from the Cycladic Islands. It has a decoration of running spirals with a ship propelled by oarsmen, surrounded by a border of wedge-shaped incisions. On the base of the handle is a triangle with a line down the centre, which is thought to indicate that the object represents the female. Opinions vary as to the meaning and usage of the objects; some believe them to be figurines, others water-mirrors. Photo: G. Kelsey

intellect, even if only indirectly and by inference. If he is to succeed in reconstructing the life of ancient man in his surroundings, he will need to employ the controlled use of his imagination. Only thus can he hope to understand the diverse mysteries of cave art, Cycladic 'frying pans' (Fig. 2), 'statue-menhirs', and prehistoric rock-carvings.

This duality of character in archaeology – of science and humanity – should not be seen as in any way a conflict of interests or a contradiction in terms. As O.G.S. Crawford put it long ago, 'archaeology is an art which employs a scientific technique'. As such it can provide one of the few genuine bridges between the 'two cultures'. In recent years there has been a trend in this direction. Indeed archaeological reports often include a whole series of specialist contributions by scientists of one discipline or another; a glance at recent volumes of the *Proceedings of the Prehistoric Society* will reveal articles devoted entirely to complex problems of bone identification, statistical sampling and similar topics.

The present age of 'scientific archaeology' is far removed from Sir Mortimer Wheeler's delightful pen sketch: 'The archaeologist wears corduroy shorts, strides about on draughty landscapes with a shovel and an odorous pipe, and is liable to be an undergraduate.' There are still many archaeologists who might be identified with this fanciful image – though the shorts have tended to be replaced in the picture by the white overall, the landscapes by the laboratory and the shovel by the microscope. In fact, of course, few archaeologists don an overall or use a microscope. Nevertheless, to the many skills and attributes with which Professor Clark (*Archaeology and Society*, p. 36) would endow the 'ideal archaeologist' must now be added an understanding of several sciences and the processes by which they can assist him. There is a growing number of archaeologists whose involvement with science is much closer to the new image. Many of those whose special interest is the study of ancient pottery or metalwork will spend part of their time in a laboratory, while environmental archaeologists will divide their time between field work investigations and laboratory analysis of the samples they have collected (Fig. 3). Others may spend as much time in a computer centre as they will in a

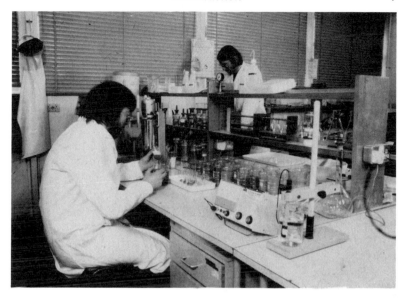

3. Part of an archaeological laboratory studying ancient environmental material – soils, mollusca and pollen. Environmental archaeology is one area where the modern archaeologist spends a large part of his time in a laboratory undertaking various scientific analyses of material recovered in fieldwork and excavation. Photo: T. Corns

library.

Strangely, although the public seem to have accepted this new image of the 'scientific' archaeologist, the questions put to the excavators by visitors to the site of a dig are much the same as they were twenty years ago. Any practising archaeologist will be familiar with the nine questions on which the chapters of this book are based. My purpose is to provide such answers as will neither confuse the reader nor compromise the archaeological truths. Most visitors to excavation sites do not care for the subtleties of excavation strategy or tactics; they do not wish to know how carbon 14 dating works or what 'thermoluminescence' means. Their questions are more direct and basic. While some relate specifically to a particular site and therefore cannot be answered in general terms, such questions as 'have you found anything interesting?' and 'How do you know what it was?' are posed so often that I have tried to answer them – the first by discussing the archaeologist's attitude to his finds and t'ır second by describing how he builds up an interpretation of the structures and features uncovered.

By the time he reaches the end of this book the reader ought to be better equipped to visit archaeological sites, to understand more of what he sees and to ask the sort of questions that will elicit informative replies.

2. Why are you digging it up?

This may not be the first question a visitor puts to an excavator, but it is one that commonly arises as conversation develops. The excavator can answer it either by referring to the immediate circumstances that brought about the excavation or by discussing the much broader reasons why he and archaeologists in general should be digging at all. Often the onlooker does not know what sort of answer he wants. He may appear satisfied with the information that, for example, the site is to be covered in for use as a car park; or he may expect the archaeologist to justify not only his particular excavation but

4. Rescue excavation in progress. Construction of the M5 motorway in Somerset revealed an important late Romano-British settlement with stone-built houses. The scene, with the machines, the earth pushed to one side, the mud and water, and the absence of carefully laid out and scrupulously tidy trenches, is typical of such rushed operations where time is at a premium. Photo: D. Miles, courtesy M5 Research Committee

all other excavations as well.

Excavations can, at least in theory, be divided into three types. *Rescue excavations* are so called because their purpose is to salvage what information they can from a site which is soon to be disturbed or even completely destroyed. In the industrialised and highly urbanised civilisations of the western hemisphere, transport systems alone result in the disturbance of existing land surfaces on a vast scale. The construction of motorways in Britain, for example, presented archaeologists with a challenge that was extremely difficult to meet, necessitating hundreds of rescue excavations (Fig. 4). In more concentrated areas, airport extensions have raised similar problems throughout Europe. Railways and canals, however, were in the main built before archaeological excavations had become commonplace. Though a mass of important evidence was thereby lost, it must be recognised that if such networks were to be constructed today the pressure of rescue work would prevent the recovery of much of the information whose loss is now mourned. In general, it is the antiquities of the countryside that are most seriously affected by the disturbance and destruction wrought by present-day transport systems. Equally potent factors, however, are condemning the earliest towns to oblivion. Many of western Europe's modern cities were once Roman towns that have been continuously occupied ever since. There has been endless building, repairing, demolition, rebuilding and destruction over many centuries. All such activities disturb or annihilate the buried remains of earlier towns. The discovery, excavation and partial preservation of Viking York is an outstanding example of redevelopment transformed from a threat into an opportunity, but not all historic towns and cities have been so fortunate. Today the pace of building and redevelopment is such that the archaeologist is under constant pressure to try to 'rescue' these now fragmentary remains by excavating them – in advance of the bulldozers – and recording the information they reveal. The creation of new towns such as Milton Keynes in Buckinghamshire carries the threat back into the countryside.

The danger may be immediate and dramatic, as when the building of the huge Amistad Reservoir on the Rio Grande in the United States obliterated at least 400 archaeological sites;

5. Research excavation inside the Saxon Shore fort at Portchester, Hampshire, directed by Professor B.W. Cunliffe. In the centre are Roman cess-pits and a hearth; at the top are medieval drainage ditches and late Saxon rubbish pits. In complete contrast to Fig. 4, the excavated areas are neat and tidy, the pace is unhurried and the site uncluttered. The archaeologist rather than the bulldozer dictates the speed and development of the work. Photo: B.W. Cunliffe

only two dozen were even partially excavated. But one of the most destructive processes in western civilisation is often overlooked because its effects are felt more slowly and occur in a much less blatant manner. This is agriculture, which in Britain is probably responsible for wrecking more archaeological sites than any other factor. Stone Age and Bronze Age burial mounds, Iron Age field systems, Roman villas and medieval villages are all disappearing at an alarming rate as the result of deep ploughing.

Since ploughing is less immediately destructive than bulldozing, the excavation of sites threatened by agriculture is usually undertaken in spite of the threat rather than because of it. This leads us to the second type of dig, *research excavation*. This is normally carried out to find the answers to specific queries or problems (Fig. 5). For example, R.W. Atkinson undertook a series of excavations at Stonehenge in order to establish the sequence of construction. Where and how he dug were largely determined by the information he wished to acquire, not by the route of a motorway or the siting of a new supermarket. Archaeologists would not choose to excavate under the severe limitations imposed by urgent 'rescue operations'; if such digs were the only source of archaeological knowledge, these limitations would impose themselves on knowledge as a whole as well as restricting excavation of a particular site.

The third and least common type of excavation is undertaken to train new archaeologists. *Training excavations* do not imply a lower standard of work, though they may progress at a slower rate. Many university archaeology departments run training excavations for their students and certain training schools, such as those at the Roman town of Wroxeter, are open to members of the public (Fig. 6).

These three types of excavation are presented here, for the sake of clarity, as separate and distinct operations, but in practice the divisions are often blurred. For example, a training excavation on the site of a Romano-British villa at Barnsley Park, Gloucestershire, was also a carefully controlled and planned research project. Where adequate notice is given of impending disturbance or demolition of a site, it is often possible to undertake a research excavation, rather than a

6. A training excavation in progress on a Romano-British farmstead at Butcombe, Somerset. Here students are learning to wash, mark and sort pottery fresh from the dig. Others will be taught excavation techniques, surveying, drawing and recording. Photo: P.J. Fowler

rescue dig. In these circumstances, it may be reasonable to run a rescue, research and training operation all in one. Thus the immediate answer to 'Why are you digging it up?' may reveal a multiplicity of reasons.

There are deeper issues implicit in such questions as 'Why do archaeologists dig at all?', 'Why do they need to dig?' and, in the final analysis, 'Why archaeology?' Some of the more cynical members of the profession might claim that they dig because they earn a living that way, but most would admit that they do it because they enjoy it. There are times when digging is not entirely enjoyable – mid-winter in England and midday in Jerusalem spring to mind. But these moments are more than compensated for by those other times when discovery and detection lift the spirits and challenge the mind.

It would perhaps be more convenient, and it would certainly be more comfortable, if one could carry out archaeological detection without actually having to dig the soil, but generally speaking one cannot. There are many aspects of man's past, even in historical periods, which either have no written record or are insufficiently or incompletely recorded. For example, we have learned much about everyday life in a colonial fort in North America from the excavations at Louisbourg, and about everyday life in medieval England from excavated villages like Wharram Percy and North Elmham (Fig. 7). By far the greater part of man's existence has, however, been in a world totally without written records. For the whole of this vast span of time, the only evidence for the development of man's religions, arts, technological skills, social customs, methods of warfare and so on – in fact, for man's progress as a social and spiritual being – is that which survives in the form of artifacts, structures and deposits. In most places, and for most periods in the past, these will have survived only because they are buried beneath the ground. If we are to acquire the information they offer, there is no choice but to excavate them.

The basic query 'Why archaeology?' has often been debated. Two fundamental values seem to me to justify its continuing existence. There can be few other disciplines or fields of study which offer such a broad education. Archaeology is closely related to anthropology, ethnography and sociology; but the student of the past must also understand the philosophy and the skills of the chemist, the physicist, the geologist and the zoologist, to mention only exponents of the more obvious sciences with which he has a working relationship. He does not need to know in detail how C14-dating is calculated or precisely how his metal artifacts will be examined and analysed, but he does require some knowledge of how the scientist thinks and what his capabilities are. However, we must not place too much emphasis on this aspect of archaeology, for fear of underestimating the importance of the humanities in the study of the past. In reconstructing an ancient society, the archaeologist is concerned with much the same facets of human behaviour as the student of a modern society – and think how many fields of specialisation there are for such a student today. For the past, there is no such proliferation of specialists. There are, of course, ancient historians, philosophers, linguists and epigraphists; but these are concerned only with historical societies.

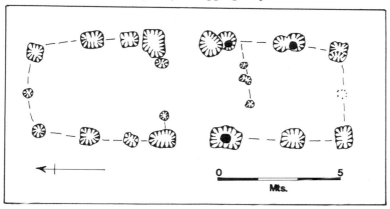

7. The plan of a three-roomed timber house (late eleventh/early twelfth century) at North Elmham, Norfolk. Although some of the village history is known from written records, information about the form and construction of its Saxon and medieval houses has been recovered only by very extensive excavation. After P. Wade-Martins

In the field of prehistoric studies, archaeologists may specialise in pottery, architecture, stone tools or metalwork, and some specialise in the broader aspects of ancient societies: art, religion, funerary rites, subsistence economy and indeed the structure of society itself. However, these specialists are all archaeologists, and they will excavate, record, study and interpret a great deal of evidence in an area which is far removed from their own particular interests. The archaeologist thus finds himself actively engaged in the study of the whole range of human activities, both physical and mental – from those as intangible as religious faiths to others as rational as technology. A field of study which involves such diverse activities and demands such agility of mind may surely claim to offer its devotees a broad and valid education.

But what does archaeology offer to someone who does not participate in its pursuit and rarely if ever reads books about it? This question can be answered by another: 'Do we need History?' The end product of archaeology is history in the broadest sense. Archaeology's contribution to history is twofold. In the first place it supplements the written sources and provides a much fuller account of past societies. Almost all early documents were concerned with great *events*, and they give little information about everyday life or the *processes* by which the nature of daily life was changed. Archaeology, on the other hand, constantly provides evidence of processes. Thus it is archaeological evidence that contributes so much to our understanding of the way ordinary men and women lived and worked in antiquity. Archaeology presents not only a more comprehensive picture of the past but a 'living' history, which can be more easily (and quite literally) grasped and may appear particularly relevant. The fact that so much emerges from the mute testimony of ancient pots and pans adds a new dimension to the story of man, enabling it to be seen 'in the round'.

Archaeology's second contribution to the study of the past is that it greatly expands the period of man's known history. For the millennia before written records began, only the archaeologist can provide evidence. The importance of this evidence is not simply that more remote knowledge becomes available. By greatly extending the period of known history, archaeology has made apparent those broad trends and patterns in the story of man which would escape attention if only those centuries with a written record were studied. It has given history a new perspective and fostered a different approach. Since it is concerned largely with processes, it has encouraged people to look at history from this broader viewpoint, rather than as a series of separate events.

But, whether it be derived from written or archaeological sources, is History needed at all? The knowledge, traditions and beliefs which make up today's society are the dynamic end-products of history. They exist today not only because they existed, in developing forms, in the past, but because they were in *some* way recorded. Apart from historical and archaeological evidence, most records will have been in a form which cannot be understood or defined, but which may loosely, and no doubt unsatisfactorily, be termed 'human memory'. It would be foolish to suggest that if all historical and archaeological records were destroyed civilisation would immediately collapse. As long as non-historical records – scientific textbooks, research papers and the like – were exempted, civilisation would continue to function efficiently.

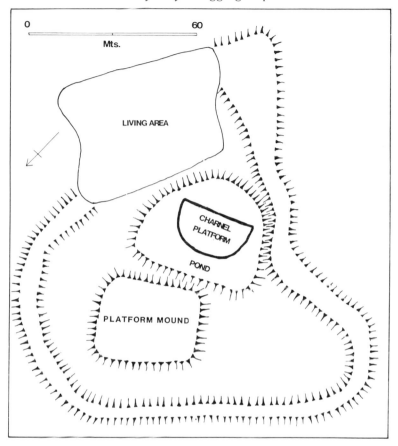

8. The plan of an excavated Indian ceremonial site at Fort Center, Florida. First occupied *c*. 500 BC, it became a major centre between *c*. AD 1 and AD 500. In the pond to the right was a platform incorporating superb wood carvings of birds and animals, and supporting the remains of over 300 corpses. To the left stood a smaller platform on which the dead were prepared before deposition on the main platform, while beyond both platforms was the contemporary living area. Much of the prehistory of North America has been recovered by archaeologists during the last thirty years. After W.H. Sears

But the quality of civilised life would be diminished, and certainly a large part of the population would feel that they had been deprived of something valuable. This impression would increase rather than decline, as human memory gradually lost

9. The zealots' synagogue inside the fortress of Masada. The site of Masada, where a group of Jewish zealots held out against the Roman army and finally committed suicide when defeat was inevitable, is of immense national importance to Israel. In many countries archaeology is promoted by the government as a means of encouraging the national identity and the concept of 'the nation'. Photo: D. Kennedy

its stored 'records' of the past. The feeling of loss would be a real one, for civilisation would have been cut off from something tangible – its roots.

If one doubts the value of history to a modern society, one has only to glance at some of those nations whose written history is relatively short. American archaeologists do not dig up prehistoric Indian settlements (Fig. 8) simply because they are there, nor have the Canadians excavated the colonial fort at Louisbourg purely as an archaeological exercise. Similarly, the care and expense lavished on the painstaking excavation and public presentation of the remains of Benjamin Franklin's house and grounds in Philadelphia is more than an investment in the tourist trade. North American society needs roots, it needs a longer and more tangible past, and the archaeologists are providing it. The same is true of Australia and New Zealand. But this feeling is not confined to young nations. Who can doubt the value and importance of the excavations at Masada (Fig. 9) to the Jews, who have a long written history? What is true of Masada and the Jews is true, in a less obvious way, of the Greeks and Mycenae and of the British and Stonehenge. Man needs a tangible past and archaeology holds the key to it.

3. How did it get buried?

The archaeologist, who spends his life studying the buried and excavated remains of man and his environment, is always a little surprised when asked this question. The answer will often appear to be obvious; yet in specific circumstances, this is a question that the archaeologist will need to ask himself. The way in which a layer or structure was buried will be a matter of considerable importance for the history of the site being excavated. The answer to the question will fall into one of two categories. The first includes all the deliberate methods of burial, and the second those that are accidental or natural.

The most obvious reply to 'How did it get buried?' is 'Because someone buried it'. Yet this is true of only a relatively small number of archaeological discoveries. By far the most common example of deliberate burial is, of course, the interment of human remains, though in some climates and in some periods of the past human corpses have been exposed rather than buried. Burial does not always imply the digging of a grave, for many peoples have used caves as sepulchres and others have built funerary chambers above ground or laid the corpse on the ground surface and then covered it with a mound of soil or a cairn of stones. Though deliberate burial of this sort normally involves a human corpse, it has often been used for other remains. Many human burials, particularly in the pre-Christian period, were accompanied by grave-goods, ranging from a single pot to thousands and a wealth of other materials too. Some of the objects were surprisingly large, like the chariots of the Marnian people who lived in the East Riding of Yorkshire and in the Paris basin in the pre-Roman Iron Age, or the furniture of the princes and nobles of ancient Egypt. But these items do not always turn up as grave-goods in a human burial. For example, the famous chariot from Llyn Cerrig Bach, Anglesey, was buried in a bog as a ritual

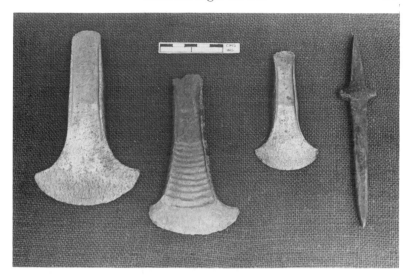

10. A hoard, perhaps the tool-set of an Early Bronze Age carpenter, found by schoolboys in 1899 at Westbury on Trym, Bristol. It had probably been hidden under a rock ledge at a time of imminent danger, and had never been recovered. Photo: G. Kelsey, courtesy Bristol City Museum

offering. The solar boats of the Egyptian monarchs were interred alongside the royal tombs, but not *in* them. Similarly, though animals may be found in graves with human remains, more often they were buried separately, and for different reasons – usually as diseased or useless carcasses, but sometimes as sacrificial offerings.

Ritual burial provides numerous examples of articles deliberately buried. From the so-called Field of Offerings at Byblos in Lebanon, for example, the French archaeologist Dunand recovered many large pottery jars crammed with bronze weapons and figurines and, less frequently, silver vessels. At the other end of the scale are the few scraps of pottery and broken bone pins found by British archaeologists in small pits dug within henge monuments of the period *c.* 2000-1500 BC. Sometimes it is difficult to identify with certainty a ritual burial of objects, and there are undoubtedly a large number of ritual burials which are at present called

11. An unusual 'hoard' of trade pots discovered at Horsetail Falls, Minnesota. They had been lost on the river bed when the boat in which they were being transported sank in the rapids. Archaeologists have begun to pay special attention to such potential danger spots as likely locations of whole shipments of early American trade goods in a state of preservation. Photo: Minnesota Historical Society

hoards. The rich hoards of goldwork from the bogs of Ireland, for example, were probably deposited for religious reasons. Some hoards, however, owe their existence to a threat to property (Fig. 10): in times of danger or insecurity, ancient man seems to have gathered together his most precious possessions and buried them. For a variety of reasons these hoards were never recovered and remain to be found by the archaeologist or, more frequently, by the ploughman or peat-cutter (Fig. 11).

The methods of deliberate burial so far described are the more glamorous ones, where rich collections of artifacts and the macabre fascination of skeletons often go hand-in-hand. Other methods are far more mundane, but to the archaeologist are just as informative. For example, although ancient man made rubbish heaps, he also used refuse pits, and every time he dug such a pit he was consciously and

12. The tell of Jericho, a completely artificial hill resulting from almost continuous occupation of the site for eight thousand years. Nomadic hunters, attracted first by the spring of fresh water, later began to settle here permanently and slowly developed a community extending over ten acres and defended by ditch, wall and towers. From this time onwards the continuous demolition and rebuilding of the mud-brick houses created a steady build-up of debris; the whole of the deposit seen in the photo is the result of human building and demolition activity. Photo: J. Rogerson

deliberately burying material. Similarly, when his living-room floor became dirty and perhaps uneven, he would cover it with a new surface in order to bury the accumulated debris. In excavating the site of ancient buildings, deliberate but unconscious burial has frequently to be taken into account. It was not simply a matter of ancient man demolishing one building to its foundations and erecting another over them. After demolition, the debris was often levelled and used as a base for the new structure. In the Near East, where house walls were built entirely of mud-brick, the resulting depth of

13. An old cottage in an advanced stage of decay. Once the windows and walls start to disintegrate and the roof collapses, plants quickly take root in the rotting debris on the floor. Photo: P. Wade-Martins

debris could be considerable.

Nothing illustrates the process so clearly as the *tells*, or artificial hills, of the Near East. The *tell* of Jericho, for example, despite tremendous erosion, is a great mound more than 15m high (Fig. 12), where once there was only a spring of fresh water. This man-made hill has resulted from six or seven millennia of construction and demolition of mud-brick buildings, together with the deposition of domestic rubbish. But at Jericho, and other Near Eastern *tells*, natural as well as human factors have played their part in burying the past. Weathering eventually reduces mud-brick to its original state – soil – and Jericho, for example, is a mound not of recognisable mud-bricks but of the material from which they were once made.

Natural factors, which play an important role in burying the ancient landscape and the man-made features on it, are the ones which puzzle people most. To many it is a mystery how anything as substantial as a masonry building can become buried beneath a metre or two of soil. Yet the early stages of the process can often be seen in the modern world. Once a building begins to fall into decay, its timber parts will soon rot, and even in a masonry building this usually means that the roof will collapse before long. Fallen, decayed woodwork and small particles of soil blown in through gaping doors and windows begin to form a thin layer of soil on the floors. Here, and in cracks in the masonry or in disintegrating wooden window-frames and sills, small plants begin to take root (Fig. 13). There follows an almost endless cycle of decaying vegetation providing a rich bed in which more plant life grows. As the walls begin to crumble, more dust and small particles of soil are swept over the site by the wind. To this process other natural factors may be added. For example, if the site lies at the bottom of even a shallow slope, soil-creep and hill-wash will gradually bury the old surface, and the remains standing on it, beneath further deposits of soil.

This process of natural decay and burial can be effective on its own. But in many cases it is assisted by human interference. The ruins of masonry buildings, for example, offer an easily accessible source of stone for further construction work. The removal of such material can rapidly

14. The experimental chalk-cut ditch on Overton Down, Wiltshire, made in 1960 to study the changes which take place over periods of time in a ditch and in materials buried within the bank. *Above* the ditch as it was after a single winter's exposure. *Below* the ditch in 1964; the shape has undergone considerable modification and the bottom has already been buried. As turf and topsoil fall in and the sides become less steep, colonisation of plants and the formation of humus may occur. Photo: G. Dimbleby

reduce the amount of buried masonry at the site, and may indeed cause the whole structure to disappear. Timber buildings suffer less in this respect, but they decay more rapidly and produce richer humus deposits, so that they are soon buried. If stone and timber buildings can disappear within decades, then obviously less substantial features vanish much more quickly. This is one of the problems being investigated today on Overton Down, Wiltshire, where archaeologists constructed their own bank and ditch and are studying how quickly the ditch is filling up with silt and debris and changing shape as its edges and walls collapse into the bottom. To compare the original ditch of 1960 with its appearance only four years later (Fig. 14) is to grasp at once the speed of the natural process of burial.

15. The inside of a bakery in the Roman town of Pompeii. The excellent preservation of this and other buildings at Pompeii and nearby Herculaneum – both destroyed by the eruption of Vesuvius in AD 79 – is due not only to the suddenness of the catastrophe but to their protection by the overlying volcanic deposits.

There are occasions when nature's haste seems positively indecent, as with the disasters which have buried whole cities in a matter of hours. A well-known example is the tragedy of Pompeii and Herculaneum, buried by ash and lava during the eruption of Vesuvius in AD 79 (Fig. 15). Recently, however, excavations on the island of Thera in the Aegean have begun to reveal a town, some 1,600 years older than Pompeii, buried beneath as much as 30m of ash and pumice in a few hours of violent natural upheaval. The centre of the island was blown to pieces by a gigantic explosion shortly after 1500 BC.

Of course, the richness of the finds at Pompeii, Herculaneum and Thera, and the remarkable preservation of the buildings, are due not only to the prosperity of these cities at the time of their destruction, but to the nature of the disasters themselves. The towns were buried so quickly that the usual processes of decay were given no chance to operate, nor were the occupants allowed the opportunity to clear their houses of valuables. Equally, the depth of the overlying deposits protected the remains from stone robbing and looting.

Deliberate burials of bodies, vehicles, hoards or rubbish may also be expected to yield finds. The very fact that someone has dug a hole with the intention of depositing *something* means that, all other factors being equal, we may reasonably expect to find something in the hole if we excavate it. Furthermore, in the case of funerary burials, ritual burials and hoards, the artifacts are usually complete. But this is not so with accidental and natural burials. A building which has been abandoned and allowed to fall into ruin will often have been cleared by the occupants of anything valuable or even useful. While it stands as a decaying shell, other people may make passing visits to it, removing anything that remains. By the time the building is finally buried beneath a mound of earth, its ruins will contain only broken fragments of pottery, food remains, useless containers and the like.

Other factors which determine the survival of ancient remains include the nature of the soil, the climate, whether the remains are organic or inorganic, and human interference with natural processes, such as mummification. These need not be gone into here. The point to be made is that the archaeologist not only asks himself 'How did it get buried?'

and 'What does the method of burial imply in terms of the history of the site?', but also 'What has been the effect of the method of burial in determining the survival or destruction of the evidence?' Only when he has the answer to this will he be able to make a balanced assessment of the evidence which *has* survived.

4. How did you know it was there?

This question need never arise in the case of the archaeological sites which are permanently visible above the ground, such as the *tells* of the Near East already mentioned. These mounds stand out so clearly on the flat plains of Mesopotamia that their artificial nature is apparent long before the visitor approaches close enough to see the mass of building and occupation debris littering the slopes and the ground below. The nearest parallels in western Europe are probably the Iron Age hillforts, which utilised natural hills but festooned them with great banks and ditches to keep enemies at bay; these now serve as clear indications of an ancient settlement. But many other types of ancient site are plainly visible to the eye. Although Britain cannot boast any remains to match the Colosseum or Pompeii, its Roman antiquities include the walls of Silchester, the fortifications of Portchester Castle and Hadrian's Wall. In the prehistoric period, Britain and western Europe produced few structures that were likely to withstand the passage of time, but among those that survived the millennia are sacred sites like Stonehenge and Carnac, and thousands of megalithic tombs and barrow burials. Some of these, now called dolmens, stand out on the landscape like primitive buildings, denuded of any covering mound that once obscured their structure; others, still well-covered by soil or stone mounds, are almost as easily spotted. But many thousands of barrows have disappeared completely and thousands more are now extremely difficult to discover. How does the archaeologist set about finding archaeological sites which do not conveniently stick out from the landscape like sore thumbs?

If he is honest, he will admit that very often he does not set about finding his sites at all; they are discovered for him. This happens in a variety of ways. Agriculture frequently brings

16. Members of a rescue excavation team battling to recover what they can of the plan of a mid-first-century Roman building, possibly the forum or market-place, discovered during construction work in London. In addition to the time limit, there is the tremendous complexity of levels resulting from long and continuous occupation of the city. Photo: B. Philp

new sites to light, as well as turning up innumerable stray finds and hoards. Many a Roman villa, for example, was first 'discovered' by the plough, while the intriguing seventh-millennium BC settlement of Nea Nikomedia in Macedonia was revealed by the digging of irrigation channels.

Quarrying, too, has been responsible for both the discovery and the destruction of ancient sites, especially gravel digging. In Britain areas so threatened are now the subject of intensive archaeological activity, as in the Thames Valley. Much of the

17. Giant graders constructing a motorway in California uncovered a series of pits and post-holes. Archaeologists are trying to excavate as much as possible of this Indian site before it is completely obliterated. Photo: Hester A. Davis

gravel removed is used for construction work of one kind or another, and this in turn frequently results in the uncovering of further ancient remains. A great deal has been learnt about Roman and medieval London from excavations conducted because archaeological remains were accidentally exposed by modern construction work (Fig. 16). Only recently a major mid-first-century building was discovered in this way and provisionally identified as London's first forum, or market-place. The construction of roads and railways also brings to light remains of ancient rural settlements (Fig. 17). Nowhere was this more vividly demonstrated than on the line of the M5 motorway in Gloucestershire and Somerset. As the initial earth-clearing progressed southwards, a string of hitherto unsuspected sites was revealed. These were mainly native

18. River erosion exposed the walls and floors of this Hellenistic-Roman settlement in Crete, enabling archaeologists to study the history of the site without excavating it. The vertical arrows on the photograph indicate the position of walls; the horizontal arrows mark the floor level. The river which was responsible for its initial discovery is also rapidly destroying the site by undercutting it during the winter months. Photo: K.B.

settlements with no stone-and-mortar structures, so that in the past the sites were less easily detected than the contemporary Roman villas. The motorway thus added a new element to the picture of this area between *c.* AD 50 and AD 400. Beneficial results have sprung from other unlikely sources. Dredging operations in California, for example, revealed many hitherto unknown early Indian sites that were covered by water, and marine archaeologists have been able to pinpoint and examine some of these. Even warfare has played its part in uncovering the past. Anyone who doubts the prospecting ability of the armed forces should consult Professor Grimes's two fat volumes, *Excavations on Ministry of Defence Sites*, which describe the archaeological excavations undertaken on sites first discovered by troops digging gun

19. A severe storm in 1866 revealed the Neolithic village (*c.* 2000 BC) of Skara Brae on the west coast of mainland Orkney. Excavation in the 1920s showed it to be a remarkable group of stone-built huts in which beds, hearths, cupboards and sideboards were all made of stone and therefore preserved. Photo: K.B.

emplacements, trenches and other military features.

Nature, too, takes a hand in archaeological discovery. Erosion may expose part of a site, often through the work of the sea, as where the breakers revealed a Viking cemetery in Deerness, Orkney, or the action of a river (Fig. 18). Violent and sudden exposure is rare, but often more dramatic. The severe drought of 1853-4 exposed the Swiss lake villages, which might otherwise never have been found and excavated, while the remarkable Stone Age village of Skara Brae, on the mainland of Orkney, was initially revealed by one of those magnificent storms that strike the island's Atlantic coastline (Fig. 19).

Much more could be said about the ways in which archaeological sites are revealed by accident rather than design, but my main concern here is to explain how the archaeologist prospects for his sites, for this is an important part of his work. Accidental exposures are largely unpredictable and beyond his control; he must make what use of them he can when they occur. But he cannot afford to wait for them to happen, because when something is revealed by accident it is invariably exposed out of *context*. Every piece of archaeological evidence removed from its original associations, from the deposit in which it was originally situated, is evidence lost, not found. The archaeologist must therefore aim to discover sites *before* they are accidentally exposed.

But where to look, and where to begin? It would be foolish for the archaeologist in search of sites just to launch himself into the landscape totally unprepared. The preliminary work in discovering new sites is done not in the field, but in the library, the archives and the map-room. The first step is to get acquainted with the geology and topography of a particular area, in other words to gain an understanding of the nature and shape of the landscape. Many archaeologists confine their search for new sites to areas where they have lived or worked for many years, because they have developed a 'feel' for them. Alternatively, a helpful start might be made by consulting maps and photographs, which will reveal a great deal about the shape of the land and the soils and rocks which compose it. Maps will also show parish boundaries, footpaths, long-established lanes and roads, all of which may reflect older boundaries or routes. Place-names often reveal the location of ancient sites, such as the Roman *cester* (camp) or the Arab *tel* (man-made mound). Other names may be linguistically significant, like the Anglo-Saxon *ingas* names (Tring, Dorking) which betray Anglo-Saxon settlements. More detailed and specific clues must usually be sought in older and less widely distributed maps or in parish records, from which the original field names of a chosen area can be gradually accumulated. Some of these names may be suggestive of earlier discoveries of building debris or foundations (Tile Field, Chapel Field, Stoney Field), while others (Kiln Field, Oven Field) may reflect the existence of kiln or destruction debris. Such field names can never be regarded as firm evidence for the existence of ancient remains, but they provide clues which, together with further research and fieldwork, may lead to their discovery.

Parish records also produce many references to stray finds of antiquities and to ancient structures which were still visible above the ground two or three centuries ago. Similar information comes from many books written in the eighteenth and nineteenth centuries, and not only from those purporting to be about antiquities. From all these sources the archaeologist may reasonably hope to discover clues to the location of ancient sites. He may also be able to examine the accessions registers of local museums, which recorded many examples of stray finds that eventually passed into their collections. Reports on previously excavated sites in the area will also be available, enabling the archaeologist to understand something of their nature, the sort of material they produced, the economy on which they were based, and the sort of locations where they occurred. All these points will help him to know where to look and what to look for.

He may now be able to take his work a stage further before starting work in the field. In neither the ancient nor the modern world do settlement patterns occur at random; indeed, the term 'pattern' implies as much. By plotting the information on to a map the archaeologist may be able to see the pattern emerging and to understand something of the rhyme and reason behind it. If he can do this, he will be well on the way to finding new sites.

All this desk work may seem far removed from walking over muddy fields in search of tell-tale scraps of pottery and flint, but it is a necessary precursor of this activity. Having exhausted the information derived from books, records and maps, the archaeologist must now see how much he can wring from the landscape itself. Today, many surveys intensively search several square miles of land in order to establish fully the pattern of human settlement from the earliest times to the present day. The results and the density of the finds are sometimes staggering. In the Tehuacan valley in Mexico an American team found over 450 sites, dating from about 10,000 BC to AD 1500. The survey was tied to an extensive excavation programme, so that subsequently twelve key sites were excavated. Intensive surveys of this kind are extremely valuable, but they are also very expensive if conducted on a large scale because a large number of archaeologists have to be in the field for a long period, in addition to the time taken to study, analyse and record all of the material and information

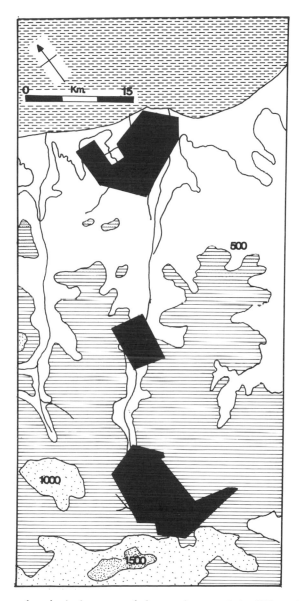

20. An archaeological survey of the catchment of the Biferno River in Molise, south-east Italy. Recognising that it was impossible properly to survey the whole area (3,000 sq. km.), the archaeologists chose three 'sample' areas which represented the three topographical regions into which it could be sub-divided. The results of the survey could then be used to estimate the likely number and position of sites throughout the catchment as a whole. After G. Barker

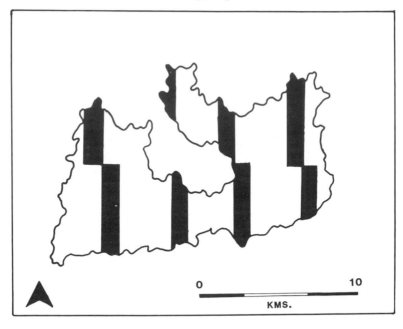

0   10

KMS.

21. An alternative approach to survey on the island of Melos. Here, a team of ten archaeologists were to survey for three weeks – a total of about 200 man-days of survey work. Since it would take about five man-days to survey each square kilometre properly, they estimated they could only cover about a fifth of the island's total area. They therefore set out, and surveyed, a systematic series of transects across the island as shown here. A total of 68 new archaeological sites were found in this sample – more than doubling the number previously known from the entire island. After J. Cherry

collected. Archaeologists have therefore developed what they call 'sampling strategies', which allow them to examine intensively only a series of samples within the general survey area. Such sample areas may be carefully chosen so as to represent the different landscapes and environments within the general area (various topographical locations, areas with different soils, access to water and other natural resources). Such was the approach adopted in planning a survey of the Biferno Valley in south-eastern Italy (Fig. 20) An alternative 'strategy' is to survey a series of 'random' strips or squares which are drawn on to the map of the area. This was the

22. An aerial photograph of a 'shadow site'. Taken from an oblique angle in order to catch as much shadow as possible, it shows an extensive area of ancient fields which can be picked out by the shadows cast by their boundary banks. These fields on Rentwood Down, Wiltshire, are probably of Romano-British date. The same system can be traced as a series of soil marks in the ploughed field on the left. The low banks of the boundaries may be traceable at ground level, but the pattern they form can be more rapidly identified and studied from the air. Photo: J. Hancock

approach adopted in surveying the island of Melos in the Aegean, where a series of long, narrow areas was surveyed in detail (Fig. 21). Using either method it is possible to get a good impression of the overall pattern of settlement over the whole span of human history, to identify changes in the pattern, and to formulate ideas about why the changes took place. Although large areas within the region will not have been surveyed at all, it is possible to predict where further settlements and sites may be found, by observing the patterns that emerge from the areas that have been intensively surveyed.

In some parts of the world, and particularly in Western Europe, survey work is greatly assisted by aerial photography.

23. This aerial view of a 'crop mark' site shows a neolithic ceremonial monument known as a 'henge' at Newton Kyme, Yorkshire. The big ditches of the oval henge show up clearly as dark arcs in the crops, surrounded by two discontinuous outer ditches, which might be of earlier date. The dark lines appear over the ditches because the crops grow more richly and ripen more slowly where they grow over the deeper soil of the ditches. Photo: D. Riley

This method reveals three principal types of site, two of which would be almost impossible to identify from ground level. *Shadow sites,* photographed from a low altitude and with the sun at a low point in the sky, are recognisable on the ground as a series of earthworks – low banks, ditches, mounds, depressions and so on (Fig. 22). From the air they take on form and relationship to one another; sometimes the destruction of earthworks is so advanced that they are only visible from the air in the conditions mentioned. *Crop marks,* where crops or vegetation are growing at different rates and producing different colouring due to subterranean features of one sort or another, are almost impossible to see from the ground, at least as recognisable patterns. From the air they show very clearly indeed (Fig. 23). Similarly *soil mark* sites are difficult to recognise and impossible to disentangle at ground level, but form a definite pattern from the air (Fig. 24). Soil marks occur

24. An aerial photograph of 'soil marks' at Ridgeway, Dorset, indicating a group of Bronze Age round barrows, which have been ploughed flat. At least six can be identified in the photograph, four of them linked together in a straight line. Similar barrow cemeteries were once a prominent feature of the English landscape, but deep ploughing has removed the characteristic mounds and very few remain undamaged. Aerial photography not only makes discoveries; it emphasises how many valuable archaeological sites have been destroyed. Photo: J. Hancock

where ancient man has introduced anomalies into the topsoil. Material may have been dug from lower levels during the cutting of a ditch or pit, or introduced from elsewhere, such as clay to form a building platform, or even stone and mortar for use in buildings. It might be thought that since aerial photography can reveal sites so easily and in such a readily understandable way there is no need for field-walking, but this is not so. For one thing, aerial photography is not as simple as it seems. Crop marks, for example, only occur under certain geological and climatic conditions, and even then may only be visible for a few days or at best a week or two. Furthermore their interpretation needs considerable care; all the features seen may not be man-made. The colouring of the crops varies, not only according to the type of subterranean feature over which they are growing, but also according to the type of crop itself and the stage of growth at the time it is photographed. Many early prehistoric communities may not have built earthworks large enough or dug ditches deep enough to produce shadows, crop marks or soil marks; furthermore soil marks can normally occur only where the land surface is ploughed at the present time. There are many parts of the world where, for a host of reasons, none of these indications of an ancient site may be expected. The uses of aerial photography are therefore limited to certain times and places.

Even in the areas where aerial photography is successfully used, it can only provide a certain amount of information, such as the shape and form of a site, the extent of the settlement, and perhaps a general indication as to its date and purpose. There are many other things, however, which it is possible to learn from walking over the site. Thus aerial photography does not replace field-walking; it is complementary to it, and certainly helps to define and limit the area to be covered and the questions the archaeologist will need to ask himself as he walks over the site.

What he will see and find then is obviously determined by a range of different factors. On many prehistoric sites there may be only a few scraps of badly weathered pottery and some handfuls of flint flakes, cores and implements. If bones are found, they may – partly depending on whether they are human or animal – indicate burials or rubbish deposits. On prehistoric sites in the Mediterranean and the Near East, much larger quantities of pottery, stone and bone may be discovered, as well as traces of structures, not only as masses of tumbled stone or brick, but as recognisable wall foundations *in situ*. Building debris will include broken-up floors, roofing material, plaster, mortar and so on. Together with the occasional brooch, coin, pin and other small items, these will enable the archaeologist to piece together a picture of the site and its history before he even considers excavation.

Probably the first thing he will establish is the broad age into which the site falls – the Old or New Stone Age, Bronze Age, Iron Age or whatever – and within this broad category he will soon be able to date it a little more precisely. Of course, he may find that the site has been occupied in several different ages and periods. Breaks in the continuity of occupation are hard to recognise, but can frequently be identified where enough material has been collected. Recognising the sudden, rather than the gradual, abandonment of a site also presents difficulties. Sometimes it may be possible to suggest the cause of such an event. For example, a mass of burnt debris, including a good many datable potsherds of a single period, would be reasonable grounds on which to postulate that a catastrophic fire had led to the site's abandonment, so that the archaeologist can add some colour to the historical picture he is piecing together. The sort of debris he finds will tell him quite a lot about the sort of buildings that once stood on the site in terms of their structure and interior treatment. Their purpose may be hinted at by metallurgical slags, fragments of votive figurines, broken quernstones, clay tablets and other finds. An archaeologist can, in fact, build up quite a detailed picture of a site from a sackful of material dumped on his desk.

If he is a good archaeologist, however, he will not be satisfied by just collecting artifacts. Having found his site and made a preliminary examination, he will return with paper and pencil, measures and pegs, to record the position of what he finds. If he is going to excavate the site, he may well save himself a great deal of time and money in this way, for he will gain more detailed information as to the location of structures and other features. The scatter of building and occupation debris usually shows a pattern, revealing where the structures stood and giving some idea as to their alignment. Similarly, different concentrations of debris may indicate which were the main buildings and which the lesser ones, and even the approximate location of specific rooms.

It is at this point in the examination of a site that he may most usefully employ methods of subterranean surveying. The first of these methods measures the resistance between two electrodes placed in the soil. This will reveal the presence of buried walls (higher resistance) and pits or ditches (lower resistance). The second measures magnetism in the soil, revealing areas of burnt clay and pits full of decayed organic material (higher magnetism). Through these methods, the archaeologist is able to pin down the location of many features on an ancient site before even putting spade to ground.

5. Have you found anything interesting?

Of all the questions posed by visitors to archaeological sites, this is probably the most common. Quite often to its followed by others in the same vein: 'Did you find any skeletons?', 'How many coins have you dug up?', 'What about brooches?' and so on. As these more specific questions demonstrate, the visitor who asks if anything interesting has been found is usually thinking in terms of items of intrinsic value and immediate appeal. Most excavators realise this and give the site's 'vital statistics': ten coins, one cremation burial and three bone pins, for example. Those who instead give a detailed summary of the site's history, or talk about some hitherto unrecognised local pottery fabric, simply reveal their own interests, which may be very different from those of the visitor. The archaeologist is intent on recovering information; the visitor often wants to know about objects. Thus the archaeologist will value, keep and study several categories of material which appear of little or no interest to the layman. Though often mystified by the excessive attention paid to pottery sherds, visitors may be inclined to give them the benefit of the doubt. So too with nails, tiles and flint blades. But pieces of clay daub and lumps of mortar are mostly regarded as just so much rubbish. Once one moves from man-made artifacts to natural remains – animal bones, mollusca, charcoal and soil samples – many visitors cannot understand why the archaeologist spends so much time and effort collecting and studying them. Archaeologists need hardly be surprised at this. Indeed, until two or three decades ago, they themselves rarely kept snail shells and soil samples, and even today there are those who pay little attention to nails, tile fragments, mortars and similar materials. Yet a great deal of information can be derived from them, some of which *will* be of interest to the layman and the excavation visitor.

25. Plan of plough marks left by Neolithic man (*c.* 3000 BC) in fields partly covered and thus preserved by a burial mound, at South Street, Avebury, Wiltshire. They represent initial cross-ploughing of land newly cleared for cultivation; the length of the longest marks suggests that the plough was pulled – probably by an animal – rather than pushed. The activity represented by these marks was also evidenced by the soil profile and the snail shells found within the soils. After J. Evans

The sight of an archaeologist carefully filling polythene bags with earth is but further confirmation to some visitors that archaeologists are, almost by definition, eccentric. After all, soil is soil – or is it? To begin with it is misleading to talk about 'soil' as if it were a single uniform material that will be dug through from surface down to bedrock; the archaeologist will collect samples not of soil but of soils. This plurality is very important. Natural causes and human activity lead to physical and chemical changes in soils; it is by studying these that the archaeological soil scientist learns something of the natural processes and human activities to which his particular site has been subjected. Occasionally it may be possible to identify materials of which all visible trace has vanished. For example, American archaeologists excavating at Natrium, West Virginia, found a series of what appeared to be grave pits, though no bones could be found in them. Analysis of the soil, however, showed a very high phosphate concentration, indicating the former presence of bones subsequently destroyed by the acidity of the soil. More often, a careful study of the physical composition of a soil reveals information about the weathering to which it has been subjected (and hence about climate), the sort of vegetation which grew in it (woodland, heath, grassland), and the way in which the soil was deposited (by water, wind or man). It can also indicate human interferences with the soil and the form they took. A few years ago, a Neolithic barrow at South Street, Avebury, in Wiltshire, was excavated. By studying the soils beneath it, which had been preserved there for 4-5,000 years, the excavator was able to identify two separate phases of agriculture, each followed by a fallow phase. As it happened, he was also able to discover the marks left by the ancient plough (Fig. 25). Here, the study of the soils was producing information about the history of the site and of agriculture itself. Sometimes more can be learned about the function of a site from soil analysis. It is possible, for example, to identify soils which have at one time been mixed with quantities of animal dung; this is obviously helpful in understanding the uses to which various parts of an ancient farmyard were put. But valid conclusions on these lines can only be drawn where soil samples have been systematically taken and analysed. A remarkable example of what can be achieved where this has been done is to be seen on Dartmoor in south-west England. Preserved on the moorland are large numbers of prehistoric settlements, land boundaries and fields, mostly belonging to the period *c.* 2000-1000 BC (Fig. 26). Painstaking chemical analysis of the buried soils in these derelict fields has allowed archaeologists to begin to piece together the way in which the

26. Plough-marks left by an ancient ploughman, and buried beneath peat, have been discovered by archaeologists excavating ancient field-systems on Dartmoor. Together with soil-analysis and a careful study of the whole buried landscape of fields and settlements, they tell us much about early farming. Photo: A. Fleming

field systems were used for rearing sheep and cattle. This is possible because sheep and cattle behave quite differently, and in particular deposit their dung in quite different patterns within a field. Detailed and extensive soil analysis, particularly for phosphorus, can identify these patterns and therefore identify the animals for which particular fields were set aside.

A sample of soil will consist of more than just earth, of course. It will often contain tiny fragments of several sorts of material such as charcoal, fibres, decayed mortar, small stones, pebbles and bones. In addition it may include small land mollusca (snails) (Fig. 27) and, in certain soils and under favourable conditions, pollen grains. The range of information provided by all these additional pieces of evidence is remarkable. Pollen analysis alone reveals a great deal about ancient vegetation and climate, and can be invaluable in building a chronological framework for the past (see Chapter

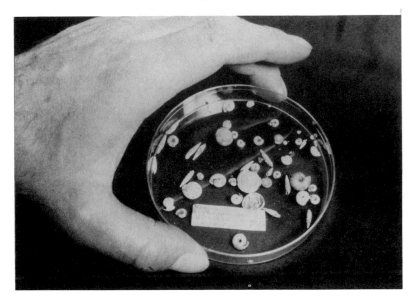

27. These tiny land snails have been recovered from a sample of soil taken on an archaeological excavation. The identification of the different species present, and their relative quantities, will provide valuable information about the natural environment at the time in which the soil deposit was accumulating. Photo: T. Corns

7). Here, for the sake of example, another one of the materials, mollusca, will be discussed in more detail.

Land snails for the most part provide the same sort of information as soils; very often the joint evidence of mollusca and soils can be used to reconstruct a picture of the climate and vegetation of the ancient world. At the South Street long barrow at Avebury, for example, the archaeologist was able to confirm his interpretation of the soil profile by a study of the land mollusca, which showed a change from shade-loving species to grassland species (Fig. 28). Apart from snails which prefer to live in open grassland and others which prefer woodland, there are also species which like marshy conditions, and yet others which prefer to make their homes in ditches. The collection and study of snail shells can thus reveal quite a lot about the immediate environment of an ancient site, and where a stratified sequence of snail remains can be found it is

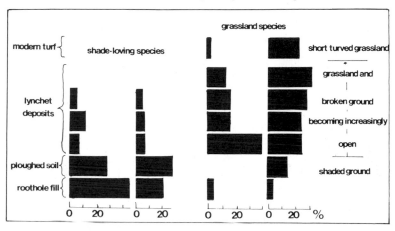

28. A simplified diagram to show how a comparative study of the snail shells found in successive deposits of soil can demonstrate changes which have taken place in the pattern of vegetation on a site. On the left, the four successive soil deposits are listed; on the right, the archaeologist's interpretation of the evidence in terms of changes in vegetation. In the centre, four species of snails are represented – two of a shade-loving type and two of an open grassland type. The numbers of shade-loving snails drop rapidly in the soil of the lynchet deposits, which accumulate at the edge of a cultivated field, and the number of grassland snails increases correspondingly. Based on J. Evans

obviously possible to detect changes in that environment, whether they be due to man or nature.

Land mollusca have never been regarded as a major foodsource as have marine mollusca (shellfish), which for the most part provide the archaeologist with information of a totally different sort. This is mainly of an economic nature, concerning shellfish utilised for food and the relative popularity and availability of the different species. Further information can be gathered by expert examination of the shells. It is possible, for example, to get some idea of the actual quantity of meat yielded by the different species – and to compare this with the volume of meat obtained from domesticated and wild animals – and also to learn something of the methods of collection. It can even be established at which season of the year the shells were gathered.

By far the best sites for analysis of this sort are the 'shell

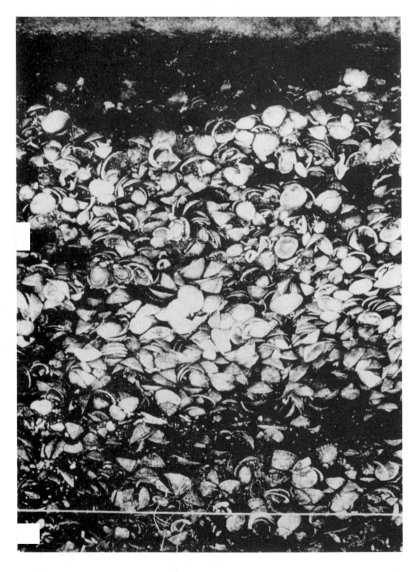

29. A section through a shell-midden on the island of Oronsay in the Hebrides. Hundreds of thousands of sea-shells, mostly limpets, make up the bulk of these great rubbish dumps left by prehistoric hunters 7,000 years ago. Photo: P. Mellars

middens' – huge rubbish tips accumulated over decades, sometimes centuries, by primitive people who lived by a mixture of hunting and fishing. Shell middens occur at coastal locations in many parts of the world, and normally contain millions of shells, as well as animal and fish bones (Fig. 29). Despite the enormous numbers of shells, careful analysis has shown that the shellfish often contributed no more than 5 per cent to the annual diet of the people who created the midden. The much scarcer bones of fish and animals, including sea-birds, in fact represent the major sources of meat for these. All this information helps to create a much more accurate and detailed picture of early hunter-gatherer people living close to the sea.

More rarely, mollusca provide insights into other aspects of ancient life, such as the use of shells as necklace beads and simple decorations, and their appearance as cult objects, as with the deposit of painted shells found alongside the famous Snake Goddess in the 'temple repositories' at Knossos in Crete. Conch shells seem to have been used in antiquity as both musical instruments and ornaments, but suitable specimens must have been difficult to obtain and may well have been objects of trade. Certainly conches discovered at some of the ceremonial centres of the Hopewellian culture of the American Mid-West must have been taken there from the coasts of Florida. Other sorts of shell and shellfish were also traded (Fig. 30). The masses of oyster shells in Romano-British towns and villas, for example, are indicative of a food-producing industry, and the shells of *Murex trunculus* from sites around the Mediterranean are evidence of the prolonged popularity of purple dyes for cloth. Shells are also a useful source of material for carbon 14 dating of ancient deposits (see below, page 90), since shell absorbs comparatively large quantities of carbon dioxide – and hence carbon 14. In addition, some mollusca species are now being identified as index species, which only appear in certain places at certain times. *Helix aspersa*, for example, seems only to have been introduced into Britain in the Roman period.

Compared with this wide-ranging information derived from mollusca, evidence yielded by animal bones may seem rather dull and limited. It is true that in the past animal bones were

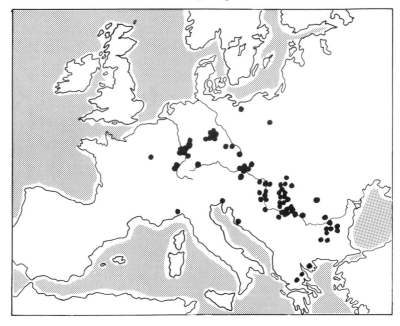

30. A map showing the distribution of *Spondylus* shells in ancient Europe. These were obtained from the Mediterranean and traded, particularly along the River Danube, deep into central Europe, where they were used by early farming communities to make necklaces. This is a particularly good example of shells being used as evidence for both trade and trade routes, which it would be hard to document from other sources. After S. Piggott

often used for ritual purposes – for figurines, maces and, indirectly, in sacrificial ceremonies – as well as for the manufacture of bone pins, awls, pendants, needles and gaming pieces (Fig. 31). Most of these items are regarded as finds in their own right. The mass of animal bones from an excavation, however, will yield information concerned almost entirely with subsistence economy.

A collection of such bones will initially indicate the range of animals available to the occupants of a site (Fig. 32). Old Stone Age sites will reveal bones of wild animals only, while those of the New Stone Age and later times will be largely remains of domesticated animals, with smaller and varying quantities of wild animals that were hunted. The next step is

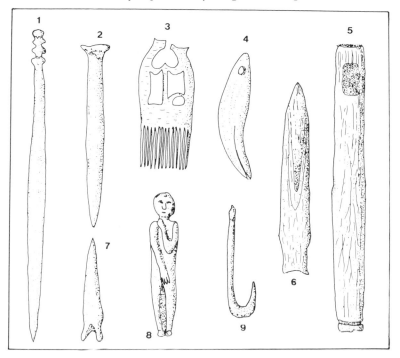

31. Artifacts made from bone and antlers by Iroquois Indians of New York State: 1 notched awl; 2 punch; 3 comb; 4 pendant; 5 whistle; 6 spearhead; 7 arrowhead; 8 figurine; 9 fish-hook. The remarkable variety of objects serves as a reminder to archaeologists of what may have been made by other prehistoric peoples out of wood, which would not have survived. After A. Parker

to try to place these animals in order of numerical importance. One cannot, of course, assume that if forty cow bones and twenty sheep bones are found, there were twice as many cows as sheep on the site. The zoologist must try to calculate the minimum number of individual animals present in any single group of bones. This is done by counting the number of examples of a distinctive but common bone – such as a femur (thigh bone). Since animals each only possess one left and one right thigh bone, if there are 26 left and 29 right thigh-bones in the sample the minimum number of animals represented must be 29. The number of bones discovered is usually far greater

32. Archaeology students at work in a laboratory devoted to the study of animal bones. The containers on the wall hold the carefully cleaned, sorted and colour-coded bones of modern animals of known species, age and sex, which can be used to compare with the bones coming from archaeological deposits. Photo: T. Corns

than the number of individual animals the bones represent (Fig. 33). For example, excavations in 1968 inside the hillfort at Cadbury Congresbury, Somerset, produced over 1,300 pig, cattle and sheep/goat bones, but only 230 individual animals could be identified. Once the minimum number of individuals in a sample has been estimated, the basis of the animal husbandry can be established. Usually, prehistoric and ancient farmers did not breed only cattle or only sheep but indulged in mixed husbandry, and the animals were bred for a variety of purposes. To clarify the relationship between the raising of cattle, sheep and pigs, and to understand something of the purposes for which the animals were raised, the zoologist must establish the age at which they were killed and, if possible, what happened to their carcasses. The animals will be

33. A typical sample of animal bones from an archaeological deposit. Many of the bones are incomplete, either because they have been broken or because they have been chopped and butchered. Teeth form a significant, and important, part of the sample because they are resistant to decay as well as being useful guides to both age and species. Photo: T. Corns

aged by studying the development of their long bones and teeth. Broadly speaking, where animals were kept to comparative old age it can be assumed they were reared for purposes other than meat production. This will usually mean that sheep were bred for wool, and cattle for use as draught animals, and for dairy products or hides. Where animals have been bred for meat, it is important to establish what was consumed on the site and what was sold or traded elsewhere. In the rubbish pits of a native British farmstead of the Roman period, at Butcombe in Somerset, the absence of discarded bones from the better joints of meat carries the suggestion that the choice parts of the animals were either being sold in a local market or perhaps were taken, as of right, by the landlord.

Information about other aspects of ancient life can also be gleaned from an examination of animal remains; although some of this tends towards the speculative, it is both

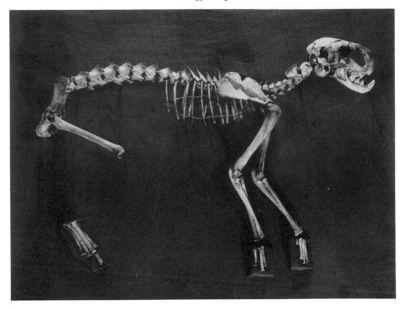

34. Skeleton of a domestic cat found beneath a floor in the Romano-British villa at Latimer, Buckinghamshire. Dated to *c.* AD 300, it is a find of some importance to the zoologist, as closely dated and almost complete remains are rare. This particular cat proved on examination to have been between six months and a year old at death. Photo: K.B.

interesting and unusual. For example, where it has been possible to estimate the varying consumption of animals, the amount of protein and vitamins constituting a people's diet can be assessed. One may go even further and suggest the sort of deficiency diseases from which communities may have suffered; where human skeletal material is available for study such hypotheses can often be confirmed.

If the zoologist is provided with suitable samples of animal bone, he can tell the archaeologist a great deal. Fortunately the exchange of information is not entirely one way. Well stratified and dated skeletal remains of animals present the zoologist with much-needed information. In some cases it may be a matter of identifying the point in time at which a particular species was introduced to a region. The domestic cat, for example, seems to have been introduced to Britain during the Roman period. An almost complete skeleton of such a cat sealed beneath a floor of *c.* AD 300 in the Romano-British villa at Latimer, Buckinghamshire, was therefore an important find, not only because it was well dated but because it provided useful comparative material for the study of more fragmentary remains of early domesticated cats in Britain (Fig. 34). A second important contribution archaeology makes to zoology is the provision of information about the early development of animals and the effects of domestication upon them. Much has been learned about the development of modern breeds of cattle and sheep from archaeological discoveries of the skeletal remains of their ancestors.

It should by now be apparent why archaeologists take such care to collect soils, mollusca and bones. Furthermore, what they learn from them is often the sort of information about the past which it might seem impossible to obtain. What weather did Britain experience in the Iron Age? What vegetation grew on the island of Crete in the Neolithic? What dietary deficiencies did the early American Indians suffer from? The answers have been supplied from a study of soils, mollusca and bones, together with other sources of evidence. To modern man these questions, and the collection of data to answer them, may seem pointless. He has little enough interest in his own natural environment, so it is hardly surprising that he should care even less about that of ancient man. But to the archaeologist, studying and trying to understand man in the past, the environment – which played a much greater role in everyday life – is a key factor.

6. Why keep broken pieces of pottery?

Potsherds – fragments of broken pottery vessels – frequently attract the attention of visitors to archaeological sites, if only because of the vast quantities which are found. All but a very few New Stone Age communities made pottery and on sites of the Iron Age and later periods it usually forms by far the largest proportion of the finds. This is because a lot of pottery was used; it was easily broken and constantly needed replacement. For the archaeologist this fragility is one of pottery's two most important characteristics. The other is, paradoxically, that it is remarkably resistant to destruction. Some poorly made pottery will crumble and disintegrate under adverse soil or weathering conditions, and it is possible to grind pottery to a powder, but most of that broken in antiquity survives for many thousands of years.

Why are these two characteristics of pottery – fragility and indestructibility – so important to the archaeologist? First, both factors ensure that large quantities of pottery survive, and that statistics may be usefully employed to study and analyse it. Secondly, the rapid turnover ensures that any changes of fashion – in shape, decoration, surface treatment and so on – appear in rubbish deposits very shortly after they are introduced. The first of pottery's several roles, therefore, is to serve as a cultural indicator. Fashions in pottery shapes, decoration and surface treatment reflect a people's artistic traditions, and perhaps other traditions too. It is thus possible to recognise communities that share a common tradition by their use of similar styles and shapes of pottery. In this way the archaeologist is able to bring together dozens, even hundreds, of ancient communities and identify them as belonging to a single culture. He will not rely entirely on the evidence of pottery, of course, but will look for other common traditions – architecture, weapons, tools, social organisation, funerary rites and so on. The basis of his cultural grouping, however, and the

35. A Food Vessel, used as a cremation urn, from Bishops Waltham, Hampshire. After P. Ashbee

first indication that a cultural grouping exists, will almost invariably be the ceramic remains. The importance of pottery in this connection is demonstrated by the number of ancient cultures which archaeologists named after distinctive pottery products such as Beaker and Food Vessel (Fig. 35). This practice is gradually being abandoned by archaeologists as it is recognised that some types of pottery might have been acquired or used by various groups of people whose material belongings had little in common otherwise. 'Beakers' are a

36. A finely decorated Beaker found at Eriswell, Suffolk. Courtesy Museum of Archaeology and Ethnography, Cambridge. These two types of vessels (Figs 35 & 36) were originally thought to be used by two separate but largely contemporary groups of people who occupied the British Isles in the period *c*. 2000-1500 BC. They were therefore dubbed the Beaker People and the Food Vessel People. The labels indicate the important role that pottery has played in indicating cultural groupings.

particular case in point. These very attractive drinking cups (Fig. 36) were once thought not only to represent a common culture but a common people (the 'Beaker people'), who had spread widely through central and western Europe. Recent studies have suggested that the vessels might represent a 'fashion' which was popular in Europe in the centuries around 2000 BC and was adopted by many different groups of people with a wide variety of material cultures. Another suggestion is that the 'Beakers' and some of the burial goods found with them were widely admired as status symbols. But the case of the Beakers and some other instances of pottery types which crossed cultural boundaries should not detract from the general value which pottery still has as one of the prime indicators of cultural groupings.

It follows that, if a common culture among ancient communities can be recognised on the basis of the pottery used, intrusions into that culture should be recognisable in the same way. Thus pottery can be useful in identifying historical events or processes, such as invasion, migration and trade. In Palestine, for example, the arrival of new peoples at the end of the third millennium BC is marked by the appearance of some very distinctive pottery. The wide range of attractive shapes and the painted and burnished decoration of the preceding periods are abruptly replaced by a limited repertoire of ugly, flat-based vessels, decorated only with incised or combed cordons of straight and wavy lines. Changes in the rest of the material culture, especially in metalwork, together with changes in burial customs and religious rites, all point to an important new element in the population. A similar combination of evidence, again dominated by highly distinctive pottery, marks the arrival of Anglo-Saxon settlers in fifth-century Britain. In both cases, the pottery is so different from that in use previously that the arrival of new people seems certain.

Pottery alone cannot be taken as final and irrevocable proof of an ancient migration; migrant peoples will reveal themselves in other ways too, as we have noted. Where anomalous pottery alone occurs, in use alongside large quantities of native pottery, the archaeologist is more likely to be looking at evidence for ancient trade. Most pottery was not traded for its

37. A group of Romano-British pottery from south-west England. Four of the vessels are native British products from kilns in Somerset and Dorset. The bowl at the centre is of samian ware, from central France. Its glossy red surface and moulded decoration contrast strongly with the British pottery and allow it to be identified immediately. Samian ware can be dated very closely, since it was produced in a small number of workshops in a few specialised areas. The work of each workshop is usually identifiable, and several pots made from a single mould can often be recognised and therefore chronologically linked together. Photo: G. Kelsey

own sake, but principally as containers for other commodities. Nevertheless, the more attractive the packaging the better the sales and the higher the price, and many pottery vessels traded in antiquity were elaborately decorated. The Greek figured vases traded into Iron Age Italy were probably the most elaborate of all. Imported pottery consequently stands out very clearly from the local products and the archaeologist has little difficulty in recognising it. The glossy red, often highly decorated samian ware produced in France in the first three centuries AD, for example, is easily distinguished in any assemblage of Romano-British pottery, even when British imitations of that style are present (Fig. 37). Sometimes, however, imported pottery is not so readily identified; this is frequently the case when we are dealing with trade within a

38. This Mycenaean pictorial vase, showing a chariot pulled by two horses and carrying two men, was found in Cyprus, along with many more of the same kind. Others vases of similar style and period have been discovered in Greece. Chemical analysis suggests that the great majority were probably made in southern Greece and exported to Cyprus. This particular vase is thought to be one of the few that were produced in Cyprus. Photo: H. Catling

single culture. Regional variations may be sufficiently clear for the identification of traded vessels, but this is not always so. There is the classic example of the Mycenaean pictorial pottery found in Cyprus (Fig. 38). Was it made in Greece and exported to Cyprus, or vice versa? On the basis of style and motifs, a satisfactory answer has never been provided; but with the use of scientific aids archaeologists have obtained the information they sought. Examples of these pottery vessels were analysed for their chemical composition, and the results compared with similar analyses of clearly indigenous pots of various types from many locations in the Aegean and Cyprus. In this way it was possible to show that most of the pictorial vases were made in Southern Greece and exported to Cyprus, although a few were made in Cyprus itself.

A stylistic analysis had earlier been made of the Mycenaean pictorial pottery, even though a solution to the problem of its origins was never reached by this method. But sometimes pottery may be so simple in style and decoration that it is not possible to use the stylistic approach. In such circumstances only a physical analysis of the pottery can provide evidence for trade. Instead of examining the chemical composition of the pottery, it may concentrate instead on its geological content – the tiny grits which have been included in the clay, whether deliberately or accidentally. Using this method of analysis, Dr Peacock has been able to demonstrate a remarkable trade in pottery which was made in southern Cornwall and distributed over distances of nearly 200 miles as long ago as 3000 BC. He has also provided evidence of other specialist potteries operating in the south-west nearly 3,000 years later.

Such information not only demonstrates much wider trading contacts in the distant past than had previously been suspected, but also adds to the archaeologist's knowledge of the economic basis of a community. Even without reference to the geologist or the chemist, he can begin to learn something about pottery production methods and the role of the potter in society. A careful examination of pottery sherds will usually reveal whether a pot was coiled, made on a slow wheel, or thrown on a fast wheel. This will give some indication as to whether the community possessed specialist potters – since fast wheels at least are usually the property of specialists – or if each household made its own pots. Dr Peacock's work on Cornish Neolithic pottery has demonstrated the dangers of assuming that handmade pottery is always the work of non-specialists. Unless the actual pottery works are found and excavated, as they sometimes are, any estimate of the size and importance of a particular pottery must be based on the known distribution and popularity of its products. This will usually mean a detailed examination – chemical, geological or of a more

39. The beginnings of a type-form series, where the archaeologist will identify all the various pottery forms (or shapes) and, using the evidence of stratified examples, try to place the forms into their correct chronological order. In this case, Romano-British pottery in two different fabrics has been sorted into its main type-forms before these are in turn sorted into more precise order. Photo: G. Kelsey

general kind – of the pottery's fabric. The archaeologist can often carry out this more general sort of examination himself, identifying the principal characteristics of the pottery's products: surface treatment (glazes, slips, washes), texture (hard, soft, sandy, smooth), inclusions (different types and size of stone particles) and basic colour of the material. Together these characteristics enable the archaeologist to identify different fabrics, and build a whole group of these into a type fabric series. By comparing these sample pieces with pottery sherds from other excavations he can begin to plot the distribution of the different fabrics and, where kilns have been excavated, to relate the fabric to particular kilns. He will then be able to take this one stage further and organise a parallel type form series (Fig. 39), showing which pottery shapes are made in the various fabrics. This may involve many years' work, but in the long term it produces a fascinating picture of how local potteries vied with each other for markets, the ways in which they specialised in certain types of vessels, and how sometimes one pottery prospered at the expense of another.

40. Two large clay vessels found in an Early Bronze Age settlement of *c.* 2300 BC near Myrtos, southern Crete. *Above* a spouted tub of the type used for the pressing and separation of olive oil. *Right* a pithos or large jar possibly used for storing oil (note the imitation overspill in paint), but also useful for storage of other commodities. Vessels like these throw light on both the pottery industry which produced them and the economy in which they were used. Photo: P. Warren

As well as supplying economic information about the industry itself, pottery also throws light on other parts of the economy. First, something can be learned from examining the functions vessels were intended to perform. Much pottery was simply kitchenware, but even pie-dishes, tankards and stew-pots provide some indication of food sources and the way in which they were utilised. Churns and strainer jugs are even more specific in this respect. On a more commercial footing, there were great vats and storage jars used in the production of oil, wine or dyes (Fig. 40). Although it is difficult to distinguish an oil jar from a wine jar, other discoveries on the site, such as seeds, pips and presses, may suggest an identification. The quantity of such containers found in a house may be a useful pointer to the economic basis on which it prospered.

Useful and interesting as all this information may be, it is of little significance compared with pottery's major role in archaeology – the provision of a reliable chronological framework. In the study of the past, time is obviously a most important dimension; to bring order into chaos some sort of proved sequence is necessary. Once we reach back beyond written history, the framework must be constructed around

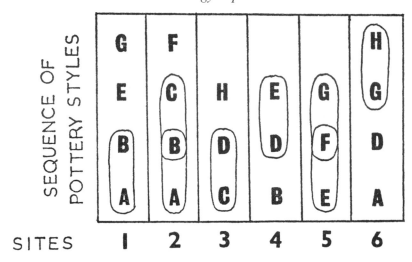

41. A simple diagram showing how a long pottery sequence can be built up from a series of short and incomplete sequences from many sites. The letters A to H represent eight different pottery styles, and the numbers 1 to 6 represent six excavated sites. The stratified pottery sequence from each site is represented by the vertical columns of letters. Although no single site produced more than three of the styles in the correct sequence, the whole sequence from A to H can be correctly identified by the overlapping of the sequence on the other sites. The keys areas of overlap, which allow the whole sequence to be established, are ringed. After K.B.

something other than historical events or calendars. The only material that occurs in large quantities almost universally is pottery, which will quickly register changes in fashions of decoration and design. It is thus the obvious material with which to construct a chronological framework.

The principle is simple enough. From a succession of superimposed levels on an archaeological site will come a series of groups of pottery. These will reveal differences one from the other, and each group will probably contain some types of pottery peculiar to that group. Distinctive pottery of this kind can be compared with that found in sequences on other nearby sites. In this way limited sequences from several different sites can produce a longer sequence applicable to the whole region and into which future finds may be fitted. A simple diagram illustrates how this system works (Fig. 41). Parts of the

42. Modelled and decorated projections from early pottery bowls found at Puerto Hormiga, Panama. The various decorative techniques, distinctive sand-tempered fabric and associated fibre-tempered pottery, all suggest that contacts existed with the south-east United States in the early third millennium BC. Photo: G. Reichel-Dolmatoff

sequence, or elements within it, will probably need to be clarified by further detailed study, for many changes in pottery styles and shapes took place over a long period of time rather than a short one.

Once a regional framework has been established, two further steps may be taken. Within the region, the much rarer stratified finds of other types of artifact – bone pins, bronze tools or weapons, brooches, figurines etc – may be placed in the framework, because they will have been found alongside pottery whose position in the sequence is known. Beyond the region, chronological links will be established with areas where different pottery styles were in use. This will depend to some extent on contact at the fringes of the regions and to some extent on the probably rare exchanges of pottery vessels as objects of trade or as gifts. Largely, however, it will depend on the evidence of influences from one region affecting the development of pottery styles in another (Fig. 42). It was in this way, with a framework supported at various points by the scarcer evidence from other types of artifact, that during the 1920s Gordon Childe was able to construct a comprehensive chronological framework for prehistoric Europe.

Although Childe gave approximate absolute dates to his framework, his chronological table was essentially a relative one; that is, it gave the order in which cultures succeeded one another rather than when the dates of the successions took place. Chronological frameworks based on pottery are still in essence relative, even though they can now be given reasonably precise time-scales based on several sorts of evidence (see Chapter 8). Pottery itself, however, may in the future be able to offer direct evidence of absolute date, through the technique of thermoluminescence dating.* It is too lengthy a process to be used on large quantities of pottery and at present is subject to errors which are imperfectly understood. Nevertheless, it seems likely that before long absolute dating will be added to the several contributions that pottery makes to the study of the past.

---

* This measures the stored-up radioactive energy in clay pottery and calculates how much time has passed since the clay was fired and the energy build-up began.

7. How did he die?

The sight of an exposed human skeleton on an archaeological excavation always arouses particular interest among visitors. They may initially enquire the sex and age of the individual, but it is usually not very long before they want to know about the cause of death. One often senses a scarcely disguised hope that 'foul play' will be the answer, and that they will be treated to a detailed blow-by-blow account of the dreadful deed. Yet I like to think that this curiosity is human rather than morbid; the excavation of a human skeleton provides a far more immediate and intimate link with prehistoric or early man than the uncovering of any number of impressive buildings or fascinating objects. Although it is often impossible for us to answer the question 'How did he die?', the careful and detailed study of skeletal remains often enables us to answer the infinitely more important question 'How did he live?'.

When a pathologist (or, more accurately, a palaeopathologist) is presented with a human skeleton, the first thing he will do is read the archaeologist's report of the circumstances of burial and discovery. On the one hand, such circumstances may point to possible avenues of enquiry; for example, the discovery of the bodies of a man and woman beneath the floorboards of a house outside the Roman fort at Chesterholm immediately raised suspicions of foul play. On the other hand, circumstances may also offer simple explanations of apparent anomalies; a burial which has been accidentally disturbed at a later date may very easily have substantial parts of the body missing, but the missing head or limb will have no significance in terms of cause of death, severe injury, or even unusual funerary practices. In addition to this sort of information the pathologist will also find it useful to know what, if anything, was found in the grave along with the skeleton (Fig. 43). Grave goods deliberately placed with a burial may provide clues to the status or even the occupation of the deceased, and the

43. Two Anglo-Saxons enjoying a joke? Skeletons like these, found in a barrow at Wigber Low, Derbyshire, always arouse great interest among the public. The presence of weapons, like the spearhead (above the head on the right), the knife (at the waist of the body) and the great iron sword (between the two) inevitably leads to speculation about foul play. In fact, it was quite normal for pagan Saxons to be buried with their weapons. Photo: J. Collis

pathologist may be able to confirm or add to this evidence.

When pathologists begin their examination of a skeleton the first thing they will usually be able to establish is the sex of the person. There are several parts of the body where male and female characteristics are most easily distinguished, in particular the skull and the pelvis, and taken together these usually provide a reliable indication of sex. Equally, it is relatively simple to establish the person's height. The first major problems arise with estimating the age at death, and the fact that we speak of *estimating* this figure indicates at once that it is rarely possible to be precise, and in dealing with mature adults it is impossible. By the time a person reaches the early twenties, all of the growth changes which visibly affect their bones have been completed. For young children the eruption of various teeth provides a good indication of age, and for people in their later teens the fusion of the epiphyses to the ends of the

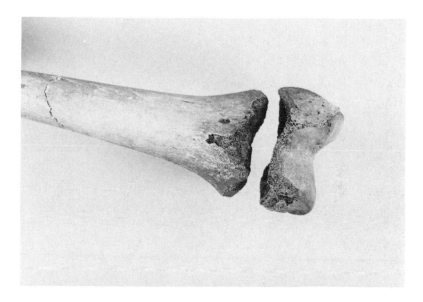

44. The end of a thigh bone, showing the unfused epiphysis; by the age of twenty the two pieces of bone will be fused together. Together with dentition, this provides a very close and useful indication of age in adolescents. Photo. T. Corns

long bones gives an instant guide to age (Fig. 44). But the eruption of wisdom teeth in the early or mid-twenties provides the last clear guide to the age at death. Thereafter, pathologists rely heavily on their estimation of the years of wear on teeth and the degeneration of other bones in the body to provide a broad estimate of whether a person was a young, mature or aged adult at the time of death. Often they can be given only very approximate ages, say 'between 35 and 50', or 'over 50 years of age'. The latest research, however, holds out hope that we shall be able to employ at least two new techniques to provide more accurate ages-at-death for adults. One of these studies the build up of tooth enamel and the other the density of blood-carrying channels (osteons) in bones. The latter technique has already been applied to a group of Anglo-Saxon skeletons from Oxfordshire and suggests that traditional methods of estimating adults' age-at-death have tended to under-age them.

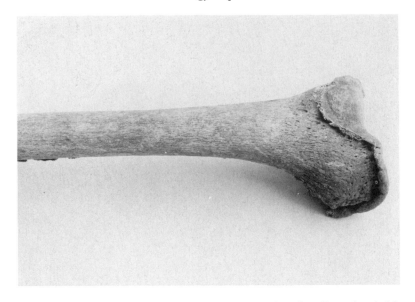

45. The end of an old man's thigh bone, showing the effect of arthritis which must have been painful if not crippling. This particular bone comes from a medieval burial in Yorkshire. Photo: T. Corns

At one time, archaeologists were content once they had been told the sex and age-at-death of an archaeological skeleton; these days they are not so easily satisfied, and will expect their pathologist to be able to say something about the person's general state of health and about the diseases and injuries from which he or she suffered in life. It may be possible to go further and use this information to say something about the person's living conditions, work, diet and, lastly, cause of death.

The general state of health of a person can usually be identified from three sources of evidence. The degree and location of osteo-arthritis will give some indication of the strains and stresses under which a person lived, and the extent to which the body stood up to these strains (Fig. 45). Dietary deficiencies in the early years of life may sometimes be recognised by long-term effects on bone, particularly those evidenced by the skull. Finally, there is the evidence of the

46. The much-damaged remains of two Romano-Britons, perhaps husband and wife, found inside the settlement at Gatcombe, Avon. Despite the imperfect preservation of the bones, it was possible to estimate the age and medical history of the two people. The woman is on the right of the photo. Photo K.B.

teeth. Carious cavities and the former presence of abscesses are easily identified, and provide an accurate impression of the person's state of dental health. We can see how these various sources of evidence provide a picture of an individual's health record by looking briefly at a Late Romano-British lady found at Gatcombe near Bristol (Fig. 46). She was probably over 40 years old when she died, a woman about 5' 2'' (157 cms) in height. She suffered from a certain amount of arthritis in the spine, but not enough to suggest that she had a very hard and rigorous adult life. On the other hand, there was some skeletal evidence to suggest that in adolescence she perhaps suffered episodes of either illness or malnutrition. In her later years, she probably suffered more pain from several carious teeth than from her arthritis.

This lady's dental problems were probably due to eating sweet foods and perhaps a general intake of too much carbohydrate, but other diseases can also be recognised by the state of the teeth. Scurvy, resulting from a deficiency of vitamin C, very often due to a shortage of fresh fruit and vegetables in a diet, leads to infected and spongy gums and tooth loss, as well as other unpleasant effects. The appropriate signs can be clearly recognised in an Anglo-Saxon man found at Caister, Norfolk. A deficiency of vitamin D on the other hand leads to rickets, which in turn results in loss of calcium and hence in soft bones which may collapse and twist. The disease is most common where people live in crowded, sunless conditions, and it can be recognised in the Roman and medieval town populations of Europe. Other unpleasant and often fatal diseases can also be recognised in prehistoric and ancient populations. Poliomyelitis was diagnosed from the skeleton of a neolithic male found at Cissbury in Sussex, and tuberculosis from that of a fourteenth-century American Indian from Avon, New York State. Recently the first Romano-British case of leprosy has been identified; by the Middle Ages the disease was by no means uncommon, as the existence of over two hundred leper hospitals in England at that time should lead us to expect. Clearly, the careful and skilled examination of human skeletal remains can tell us a great deal about the aches and pains and the physical trials and tribulations which many of our ancestors underwent, but we should bear in mind that it cannot tell us the whole story. There are many diseases which leave little or no trace in the skeletal record – typhoid, malaria, cholera, smallpox, for example – and yet the historical records tell us clearly the major role these diseases have played in human history.

Diseases such as these have of course killed millions of people through the centuries, and they provide the most obvious examples of deaths for which no cause can be ascertained from skeletal remains alone. The same is true of many more violent causes of death – asphyxiation, strangulation, poisoning and the severing of an artery, to mention only a few. So when the visitor to an excavation peers down at a skeleton and asks 'How did he die?', the chances are that neither the archaeologist nor the palaeopathologist will be able to answer that question. Sometimes, however, the circumstances and the skeletal remains point quite clearly to an answer. When local Christians decided to topple some of the great megaliths at Avebury stone circle in the fourteenth century AD, one of them was foolish enough to stand on the wrong side of the stone. It fell and crushed him to death, and his body lay beneath the toppled stone until it was discovered by twentieth-century excavators; there could be no doubt about the cause of death in this instance. Equally, the effects of warfare were immediately apparent when Sir Mortimer Wheeler opened the shallow, hastily dug graves outside the gateway to the great hillfort of Maiden Castle. Gashes across the tops of several skulls were clearly caused by a weapon such as a sword or sharp axe, and the discovery of an iron catapult-head in the spine of one of the dead confirmed that in fact the Roman army was responsible for this slaughter. Earlier isolated incidents of people being shot in the back – by bow and arrow – are recorded from France, California and Dakota, where in each case the arrowhead was still stuck in the spine. Two young men of about 1400 BC were struck down by spears near Tormarton, Gloucestershire (Fig. 47). Again, the remains of a spear head, which had broken off at the tip, were found stuck in the pelvis of one of the victims, and helped explain the injuries noted elsewhere on his and his companion's skeleton. Alongside these signs of sudden death

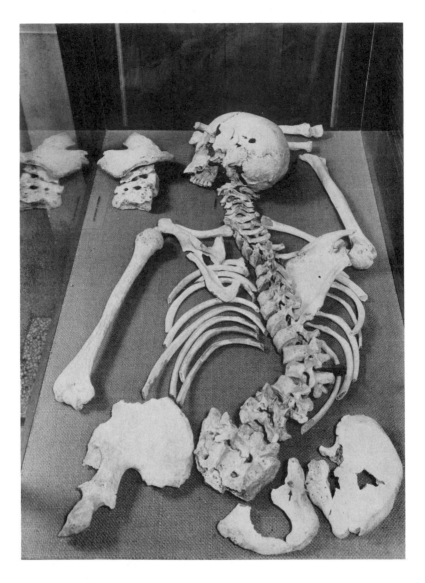

47. The skeleton of a Bronze Age youth found at Tormarton, Gloucestershire. He had been attacked and wounded in the head, abdomen and back by someone armed with a bronze spear. The wound in the back was the crucial clue, since the tip of the spearhead had broken off and remained lodged there when the body was buried. Photo: G. Kelsey, courtesy Bristol City Museum

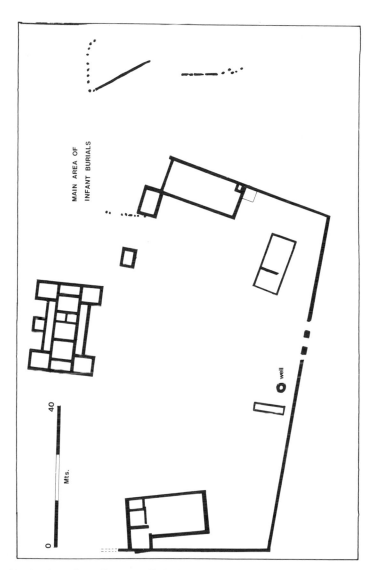

48. A plan of the Romano-British villa and its farmyard at Hambleden, Bucks. Several pieces of evidence – the discovery of a few pieces of military equipment, the building of over a dozen corn-drying ovens, and the discovery of over seventy *stili* (Roman pens) have suggested this might not be an ordinary civilian farm. The 'cemetery' containing almost a hundred very young infants is also unusual, and strongly suggests that the labour force here were slaves, among whom unwanted female babies would be disposed of at birth. After A. Cocks

we might place other cases in which we have reason to suspect judicial executions. Several Roman cemeteries such as that at Dunstable in Bedfordshire have produced skeletons of people who have been beheaded; they may be executed criminals, but we cannot be sure that the head was severed *before* death rather than soon after. What links all these cases together is that the cause of death was violent, and this violence has left tell-tale signs on the bones. The vast majority of people do not die as a result of violence, and the cause of death must usually remain uncertain, although where we can identify severe disease from bone evidence we can often be almost certain as to the ultimate cause of death.

Just as judicial executions and clandestine homicides both tell us something about the nature of contemporary society, so do many of the other pieces of evidence which we can acquire from the study of skeletal remains. The possibilities for deriving social information from bone studies are almost endless, and we can do little more than indicate some of them here. From the incidence of diseases such as rickets and scurvy we can obviously learn something about both living conditions and diet. Equally, the high incidence of dental caries in the people of Minoan Crete and Roman Europe is widely agreed to reflect the favour with which both societies viewed sweet and sticky foods prepared with honey. It has also been suggested that the Romans may have suffered from lead poisoning: their bones frequently reveal relatively high levels of lead which almost certainly reflect the introduction by the Romans of lead water pipes. Paradoxically, these pipes were intended to improve public health by providing a fresh water supply and encouraging bathing.

Social relationships and roles can also be reflected in skeletal material. We know that Roman society was based on a large population of slaves, and when we find a cemetery with a considerable number of female infants exposed (or killed?) at or soon after birth, we can plausibly identify these as the offspring of slaves. Thus the Romano-British villa at Hambleden in south Buckinghamshire, where such a cemetery was found, is likely to have been a slave-run estate centre (Fig. 48). The incidence of child-bearing, which can be estimated by a close study of the pelvis, may also throw light on the role of women in ancient societies.

Finally, we might note that skeletal remains often reflect the attitude of contemporary society to death and the dead. This is most clearly expressed perhaps by the manner and mode of burial – the construction of an elaborate and prestigious tomb, the depositing of grave goods, the evidence for funerary feasting and so on, or the absence of such features. But attitudes are also reflected in the way the skeletal remains are subsequently treated. In the case of communal tombs open for long periods of time, the defleshed bones can be treated with great respect and either left as they lie or else carefully sorted and placed at the edge of the burial area or in a side chamber; or they may be casually trodden underfoot or even shovelled out and dispersed. A good example of the careful treatment of human remains is the excavation beneath the earthen long barrow, dating to around 3500 BC, at Fussells Lodge, Wiltshire (Fig. 49). Here the bones had been sorted into neat piles and were laid out perhaps according to some predetermined order. What a contrast these remains provide to the mass of jumbled and broken bones shovelled out of the Early Bronze Age circular tomb at Platanos in Crete and into trenches dug near by. Quite different attitudes to both death and the dead seem to be implied by these discoveries, although in seeking to interpret these attitudes the archaeologist will have to move with great caution.

Information about society and its attitudes and customs can only be gained from skeletal remains where they are examined in large numbers and preferably from a single context – that is, from a single cemetery site. Much of what we have said in the foregoing pages has been written in terms of the individual, and even when the palaeopathologist has a large cemetery population to study, he will initially have to examine each skeleton separately. Only then will he be able to move a step further and produce a general picture of the whole community represented in the cemetery. As an example of what can be achieved, we might briefly summarise the picture which emerged from the study of a Romano-British cemetery population from the town of Cirencester, Gloucestershire. The remains of 362 persons were examined. On the whole they were relatively healthy people, with a low level of dental disease by

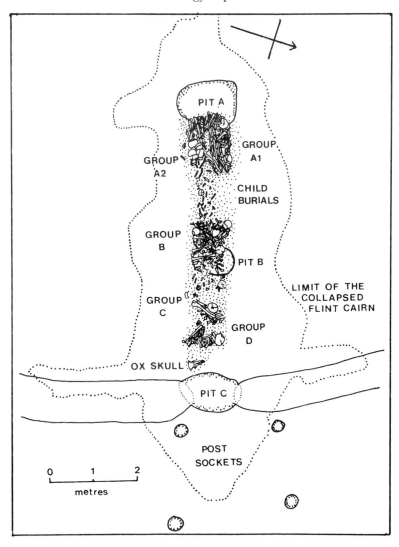

49. A detailed plan of the burial area in the Fussells Lodge neolithic barrow. The burials were incomplete and were made up of carefully sorted groups of bones taken from bodies which had probably been exposed for a long period in a mortuary enclosure. Groups A and B were the remains of adults, between which were scattered the bones of children. Group C consisted of a skull, an arm and a leg, and group D of a contracted burial, at the foot of which an ox skull was buried. Expert examination not only allowed the original number of burials to be estimated, but also provided insights into the life expectancy, health, and funerary beliefs and customs of these people. After P. Ashbee

Roman standards, suggesting a diet without too much sweet food and carbohydrate and with sufficient meat. Although the majority of both men and women suffered from arthritis, reflecting hard manual work for men and perhaps the carrying of heavy loads by some women, the condition was rarely severe. In addition to their work, the adult women seem to have averaged five pregnancies each, although almost certainly a high proportion of the offspring did not survive infanthood. To judge from both the frequency and the nature of broken ribs, physical violence – probably fights and beatings – was not an uncommon feature of life in Roman Cirencester. On the other hand, the broken bones showed no evidence of expert attention, so that it may be assumed that the people buried in this cemetery could not afford the services of one of the doctors that we would expect to find in a town as large and important as Roman Cirencester. It is possible, however, that another 'occupational group' can be identified in the cemetery. One multiple grave, sited very near the amphitheatre, contained the bodies of four adult men. All of them showed certain skeletal abnormalities and fractured bones, and it has been suggested that they may have been gladiators. However, few of the people – even the 'gladiators' – appear to have died of injuries. Those males who survived childhood had a life expectancy of forty years; women died a little younger on average, and only one in ten of either sex could hope to live beyond their mid-fifties. But by Romano-British standards this was a good age, and most of the people of Cirencester probably died natural deaths from 'old age' and various infections. Disappointing as it may be for us today, these things will have left no trace in the skeletal record.

8. How do you know how old it is?

Thirty years ago, the audience watching the TV programme 'Animal, Vegetable and Mineral' used to gasp with astonishment and admiration every time Sir Mortimer Wheeler correctly gave the date of some ancient artifact, sometimes to within a few decades. How did he do it? There is surprise, sometimes verging on disbelief, that an archaeologist can really distinguish between a piece of flower pot and a fragment of Roman pottery. That he can tell the difference between a potsherd made in the period AD 40-60 and another of AD 60-80 may seem little short of miraculous. How is it possible?

In the final analysis, archaeological dating depends on stratification, or the accumulation of a succession of deposits which have some demonstrable relationship to each other. Study of the relationships between levels or deposits will reveal which is the earliest, the next earliest and so on. It follows that the same relationship may be deduced about the various artifacts found within these deposits. On any single site, the sequence of deposits may well not be continuous or long, but a sequence can be built up by comparative studies between a whole group of sites. By studying and constantly handling the various materials making up these sequences, archaeologists come to know the forms, shapes, decorations and other features which characterise groups of artifacts at certain points in the sequence. They develop a 'feel' for pottery fabrics of different periods; it is largely this that enables them to distinguish in a second between flower pot and Roman pottery. If the archaeologist is asked what he means by 'feel' he may well have difficulty in giving a satisfactory answer, because it is something unconsciously acquired over a long period of time. His fingers have, in fact, become sensitive to differences in fabric, surface texture, weathering characteristics and so on of pottery of different periods.

It is fair to ask how the archaeologist constructs his chronological framework when confronted by the remains of Palaeolithic or Mesolithic man, who did not have the use of pottery. As long as deposits can be found in stratified sequences and yield fair quantities of artifacts, such as flint and bone implements, the system still works, though it becomes perhaps a little less precise. Changes in the type and form of stone implements, as well as in the technique of stoneworking, make it possible to recognise products of different periods. Where such objects are found in small quantities, and in strata isolated from others containing human artifacts, then the archaeologist has to resort to the evidence of natural sequences. For example, since the mid-nineteenth century, remains of early man have been placed in the time-scale on the evidence of the geological deposits in which they were found. A more precise vegetational sequence has now been identified, its general development being traced by the study of pollen grains. Those shed by living plants are remarkably tough, and under suitable soil conditions will survive for millennia. The botanist can identify the different genera, or families, of plants by their distinctive pollen grains; by comparing the quantities of each genus present in a sample of soil from an ancient site, he can draw up quite an accurate picture of the vegetation on and around the site at the time the particular soil was on the surface. The pattern of vegetation has changed many times in the course of thousands of years; it is now possible to divide the past into a number of vegetation zones, each characterised by a certain pattern of vegetation (Fig. 50). If, therefore, an archaeologist can obtain a soil sample with pollen grains, associated with an isolated deposit or even a stray find, he can place the deposit or find into one of these zones; in other words, he can date it.

Nevertheless, to say simply that an artifact dates to zone 5 or zone 6 is not entirely satisfactory, particularly to the layman. All the dating methods so far mentioned give relative, as opposed to absolute, dates. This is not to say that relative dating is unimportant or has no value. It is still the essence of understanding the past, but without an accompanying absolute chronology it is incomplete. The great value of absolute dating is that it conveys an idea of tempo in the

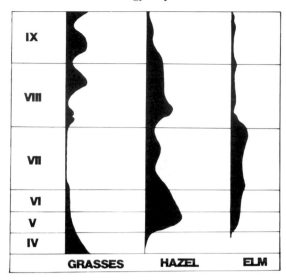

50. A simplified diagram illustrating part of the sequence of vegetation in
Jutland since the last Ice Age, as determined by pollen analysis. The growth
pattern of only three genera – grasses, hazel and elm – are shown here, and
the first three vegetation zones (periods) are omitted. If, for example, a soil
sample contained relatively large quantities of elm pollen, moderate amounts
of hazel pollen and little or no grass pollen, it could be placed in zone VII. On
the other hand, large quantities of grass pollen, small amounts of hazel and
very little elm would place the sample in zone IX. Any artifacts found in the
stratum from which the sample was taken could be placed in the same zone
as the sample. After K.B.

development of civilisation. Man has not developed at the same
speed throughout history, nor indeed throughout the world.
Think how quickly things changed in the Industrial
Revolution! To understand the way in which a civilisation
progressed it is essential to recognise changes in the speed of
development. The archaeologist needs to know, not just that a
people went through a certain stage of social or technological
development, but whether it took fifty or five hundred years for
them to do so.

Until the advance of scientific methods of absolute dating,
the prehistoric archaeologist was entirely dependent on
converting his relative chronologies into absolute ones. For
example, he could not give absolute dates for pre-Columbian

51. In this tomb group found at Abydos in Egypt, all the objects are Egyptian except for the decorated vase in the centre. This is a well-known Minoan vase type painted in the 'Kamares' style and belonging to the Middle Minoan II period in Crete. It is one of several such vases exported to Egypt. A find like this is immensely important for the dating by historical means of prehistoric Aegean and even west European cultures. This tomb group contained two seals bearing the names of the pharaohs Sesostris III and Amenemmes III, whose reigns together covered the period *c.* 1880-1800 BC. MMII in Crete – as well as other cultures in the Aegean and farther west which have links with it – can therefore be broadly dated to the nineteenth century BC. Courtesy Ashmolean Museum

remains in the Americas, or for pre-European remains in the Antipodes because they could not be fitted into the relative chronologies for Europe, Asia and northern Africa, since there were no recognisable links between them. With no scientific dating methods to resort to, the prehistoric archaeologist had but one source of absolute dates: the historical civilisations of the Near East – Egypt, Mesopotamia, Syria, Palestine and Turkey. This means that the period of absolute dating could not reach back before about 3000 BC. For the period thereafter it was a matter of demonstrating links between cultures which were historically dated in Egypt, the Levant or Mesopotamia and those of prehistoric peoples which spread out beyond them.

These links could take several forms; for the archaeologist, trade was the most obvious and perhaps the most reliable. Where goods of known date were imported from Egypt or the Levant by prehistoric peoples, a date could be given to the native products with which they were associated when found by the archaeologist (Fig. 51). Sometimes these native people would have traded with other prehistoric peoples having no direct contact with Egypt or the Levant. In this way, these people too might be given absolute dates, and so on along a whole chain of connections until dates were provided for the prehistoric cultures of western and northern Europe at one end of the chain and ancient India at the other. It has not always been possible to demonstrate a series of trading links, however; many of the links in the chain are based on less certain connections, open to more subjective interpretation. These may take the form of external influences on the development of indigenous ceramics, architecture, metalwork and so on. This sort of chronology is essentially relative and absolute dates applied to it can be, and have been shown to be, seriously in error. Obviously all sorts of factors can lead to such errors, but a general rule can be formulated by which to assess the value of absolute dates obtained by this method. The greater the time and distance between the prehistoric culture being dated and the historic civilisation providing the basis of the dating, the more tenuous are the links established – and the less reliable are the dates.

Some cultures are neither prehistoric nor historic. Those that are on the verge of becoming historic and writing their own records are called protohistoric cultures; others stand on the fringe of history, sometimes written about by historical neighbours and occasionally conquered by them. The classic example, of course, is Britain under the Romans. The archaeologist is better off when faced with this sort of situation than with entirely prehistoric peoples, but he nevertheless has difficulties in building a satisfactory absolute chronology. He will usually have a bare skeleton of historical information on which to build, such as a few important battles, occasional rebellions and imperial visits to the conquered territory. In the

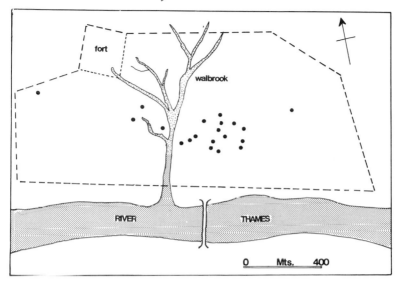

52. Plan of Roman London showing the sites of destruction deposits of the Boudiccan revolt. The dotted line indicates the position of the later Roman wall. Boudicca's destruction of Londinium, AD 60-1, left thick deposits of fire debris which have helped archaeologists in two ways. Because the event itself is precisely dated from historical sources, pottery and other artifacts found in the destruction deposits can also be given an accurate date. Also, the plotting of these deposits on a map of Roman London shows both the siting and the approximate size of Londinium in AD 60-61, only seventeen years after the Romans landed at Richborough. After R. Merrifield

case of Roman Britain, it is known that the invasion took place in AD 43, that Boudicca rebelled in AD 60-61 and that Severus came to England in AD 205 and died at York in AD 211. Some of these dates provide the framework for the history of the province, but others have an additional value, for they are associated with events which can be recognised in the archaeological record. For example, Boudicca's destruction of Colchester, London and St Albans has been clearly identified on many occasions during excavations (Fig. 52). The mass of pottery and other artifacts found in these destruction deposits can be dated very closely indeed – to AD 60-61, in fact. Others can be closely dated on the evidence of inscriptions which often record the foundation or completion of a certain building, or perhaps its repair after partial destruction. Although the Romans did not inscribe the date in so many years AD, they did something almost as useful by recording the number of times the emperor had held the consulship and other titles at the time the inscription was cut. This often indicates the date of the inscription to within a year or two, and this in turn dates pottery and other items discovered in the foundation material or in the debris resulting from repair work. Finally, coinage is an important factor in dating Romano-British deposits. From the details of the emperor's titles inscribed on the coins, relatively close dating of their time of issue can be established – some emperors being very short-lived, in any case. Where a sufficient number of coins can be found in a single deposit, further dating evidence is provided for pottery and other artifacts. Single coins, however, can be very misleading indeed; some stay in circulation for many decades, or even longer, after they are minted. These various sources of historical dating for Romano-British deposits are the backbone of the absolute chronology of Roman Britain. By using pottery, brooches and other items found in historically dated deposits to build up absolutely dated sequences of these artifacts, it is possible to date other deposits which themselves contain no direct clues to their absolute date.

This method of dating works so well with regard to Roman Britain, and indeed in similar situations elsewhere, that it has not been superseded by any of the scientific methods of dating. It is both more precise and more reliable than carbon 14 dating and, unlike tree-ring dating, it can be widely applied regardless of climate and because it is based on pottery suffers from no shortage of samples. Carbon 14 and other scientific methods of dating, however, are invaluable for the prehistoric periods, and have revolutionised the archaeologist's ideas about the absolute chronology of the prehistoric culture sequence throughout the world. These scientific methods have three great attractions. First, they are objective. While the results may be variously interpreted by the archaeologists, they derive from calculations based on observed scientific facts and measurements made under carefully controlled conditions. Carbon 14 dating, for example, is based on the fact that radioactive particles of C14 absorbed by a living organism

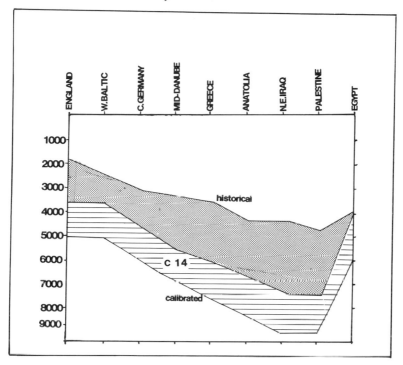

53. A simple diagram showing the estimated dates for the beginnings of farming in different parts of Europe and western Asia, showing the differences in the dates arrived at by historical cross-dating to the Egyptian calendar, by C14 dating and most recently by the tree-ring correction (or calibration) of C14 dates. It illustrates the tremendous impact which the discovery of C14 dating has had on our understanding of both the origins of farming and the pace of subsequent development. Based on G. Clarke

begin to disintegrate at a known, constant rate when the organism dies. Secondly, scientific methods of dating can be applied to isolated cultural sequences, for they do not rely on establishing links with historical civilisations. Until the introduction of C14 dating, for example, it was impossible to do more than guess at the dates of the prehistoric cultures of the American continent before the arrival of the first Europeans. A whole sequence of dates is now being built up, and in some areas, such as the Tehuacan valley of Mexico, there is a complete series of hundreds of dates covering ancient societies from soon after 10,000 BC down to the arrival of the Spaniards. The third attraction of scientific methods of dating is that they have greatly extended the span of human history for which an absolute chronology can be built. In Mesopotamia, where the earliest written documents could carry historical dating back just beyond 3000 BC, there is now a dated sequence stretching to at least 8000 BC – the span of dated history has been doubled! The same is true of many prehistoric societies that until recently were dated by vague links with the early historical civilisations. Many archaeological equations between prehistoric Europe and the civilisations of the Near East have now been shown to be false, and the chronologies built around them to be wrong.

To take the most obvious example of the impact of C14 dating, the beginning of farming in some parts of Europe and the Near East has been moved back in time, mainly on the evidence of C14 dates, by as much as 3000 years (Fig. 53). Changes of this magnitude involve more than a simple alteration of dates; they offer entirely new perspectives in prehistory and the development of civilisation, showing that the New Stone Age proceeded at a totally different tempo to that previously suggested.

The revelations first brought about by C14 dating have been followed by further surprises as we have learned to 'correct' our carbon dates. It was known for many years that our carbon dates could not be regarded as firm and final because a number of sources of error in calculating the dates could not be easily eradicated. Although some difficulties remain, one of the major problems – estimating the changing amounts of C14 in the atmosphere in the past – has been overcome by checking the carbon dates against the results of tree-ring dating. Every schoolboy knows that you can tell the age of a tree by counting its annual growth rings. A sophisticated development of this simple method now allows archaeologists to establish the age of wood (and therefore of buildings and other structures in which the wood is found) far back into antiquity (Fig. 54). In America, where the Bristlecone pine lives up to 4,000 years, the method can establish dates as far back as 3000 BC and beyond; in Britain and Europe it is already providing dates in the centuries

54. A dendrochronologist at the University of Sheffield is measuring the widths of the tree rings on an oak beam taken from a medieval building in Derbyshire. The measurements of individual rings are electronically fed into a computer which will then produce a graph showing the changing pattern of thick and thin rings. Careful matching of graphs with those from timbers of known age will allow this timber to be dated. Photo: T. Corns

preceding the birth of Christ and in time will provide even earlier dates. More important, because wood can also be carbon dated, it allows us to check the reliability of our carbon dates against the much more accurate dates provided by tree-ring counting. By making these checks not once or even ten times, but thousands of times, it has been possible to construct a chart, known as a calibration table, which allows us to read off the true date in calendar years each time we obtain a new C14 date.

An added attraction of scientific methods of dating is the diversity of materials from which absolute dates can be extracted. The archaeologist can now obtain absolute dates from wood and plant remains (including pollen), bone, shell, clay and obsidian. Few sites will not yield at least one of these sources of dating evidence. It will be some years before many of the various methods utilising these materials will be entirely reliable and accurate, and probably even longer before they are economical enough to be employed for every excavation. But by the end of this century much of the archaeologist's concern over time-scales will probably have been solved by the sciences.

The use of carbon 14 and the other scientific dating techniques is expanding rapidly, and their future potential is great indeed. The majority of excavations, however, are still dated by archaeological methods, partly for financial reasons and partly because this evidence is often more precise. When an excavator in the field tells a visitor that the long barrow he is excavating dates to *c.* 3000 BC, it should not be assumed he has a geiger counter in his hut and sits there running off carbon 14 determinations. Even if he has samples from his site, he will only get dates from the laboratory several months later. Though the date he gives the visitor may depend on C14 dates for other comparable long barrows, he will have arrived at it through the usual processes of archaeological dating. The archaeologist will have assessed the barrow itself and the significance of the pottery and other artifacts he has found, relating them to finds from barrows elsewhere. In other words, he will have built up in his mind a relative chronology for his own particular barrow. It is unlikely that scientific techniques will ever replace this aspect of archaeological dating.

9. What was it?

While many visitors may not show much interest in the problems of archaeological interpretation, they do want to know what the visible physical remains on the site – walls, floors, post-holes and so on – represent. They want to find out what they are looking at. The amount of information the archaeologist can provide usually surprises them and leaves them sceptical. How, on the basis of a few post-holes and scraps of wall foundation, can a building be reconstructed to the roof and the interior decoration be described in detail? Obviously, since each structure will differ as to its function and original appearance, no general answer can be given to the question 'What was it?' Similarly, the evidence on which function and appearance are identified will vary from one site to another, but it may be helpful to explain how an archaeologist approaches the reconstruction of an ancient building and the sort of evidence he uses.

In many ways the interpretation of architectural remains is one of the easier tasks facing the archaeologist when he begins to sort out what his evidence means. He is, after all, dealing with primary evidence – the physical remains of the structures themselves. Nevertheless, there are other factors to be considered, which together constitute the environment in which the buildings existed. These climatic, technological and social conditions will have helped to determine the sort of structures erected by an ancient people and the way in which they set about it. For example, timber would not be the main building material in a region where trees were scarce but stone was abundant; and people who could not read or write would not build libraries. The archaeologist must therefore know something of the contemporary climate, the availability of raw materials, and the social and technological development of the people concerned. He must also be familiar with other buildings belonging to the same period and culture as the

55. A modern clay-lump wall at Yaxham, Norfolk. The clay-lump walls of medieval buildings in the area have long since disintegrated and are only recognisable by a tell-tale yellow stain in the soil. When mortared together and covered with a facing of plaster, the clay lumps make very substantial walls; however, as can be seen here, the plaster covering in time cracks and falls off. When completely exposed to the weather and left unmaintained, the wall will begin to disintegrate. This type of construction is the nearest equivalent in western Europe to the mud-brick walls of the Near East. Photo: P. Wade-Martins

56. Surrounded by medieval graves, fragmentary walls and pits, the apse of the tenth-century Old Minster at Winchester can be traced not by the stone foundations themselves, but rather by the semi-circular robber trench left by those who totally demolished the structure and reused the stone in AD 1093-4. A fragment of the original foundations can be seen in the right arm of the trench. Courtesy Winchester Excavation Committee.

structures he is investigating.

Before he reaches the stage of planning the architectural remains on his site, he will usually have decided which of these remains are evidence for ancient structures. Sometimes this is a perfectly straightforward task, but it can be a difficult one, requiring considerable experience and insight. In the Near East, for example, mud-plaster floors and decayed mud-brick are only two of many structural features which may be missed altogether by an inexperienced excavator. In western Europe similar problems may arise in tracing the lines of long-since dissolved clay-lump walls, now represented by little more than a yellow stain in the soil (Fig. 55). Where buildings with stone foundations are concerned, there is obviously a much better

57. A selection of typical small finds from the site of a Roman villa. The ridged tile at the back indicates the nature of the villa's roof, and the long iron nails suggest important timberwork in the building. The patterned tile betrays the presence of 'central heating' by hypocaust, being part of a hypocaust box tile. Painted plaster on the right provides a clue to the treatment of living room walls, and the small cubes and a lump of pink mortar come from two types of floor surface. Photo: T. Corns

chance of physical remains surviving in easily recognisable form. However, the activities of later generations who robbed the ancient walls in order to re-use the stone may mean that an archaeologist will not infrequently find a robber trench where once stood a solid stone wall (Fig. 56). In addition, the excavator of stone buildings will need to examine and record very carefully any large amounts of stone rubble, which is as much evidence of the ancient structure as are the surviving fragments of standing walls and floors.

All the structural features will be included in the excavator's detailed plan of the architectural remains, from which he will begin to interpret his evidence in terms of buildings. The completed plan will represent the sum total of evidence for structures discovered on the site in situ. There

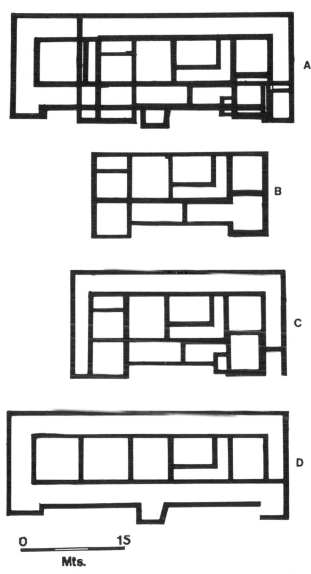

58. The Romano-British villa at Shakenoak, Oxfordshire. Plan A is the master-plan showing all the walls discovered in excavation. Plans B-D show the historical interpretation, revealing three successive buildings, none of which is identical with A. In this sense, the master-plan shows a structure which never existed. After Brodribb, Hands, Walker

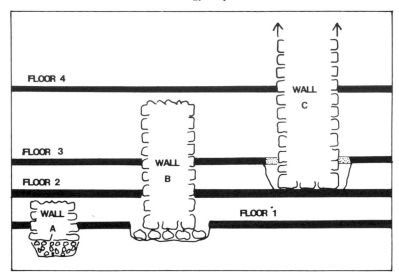

59. Diagram illustrating the interpretation of an excavated building in terms of its architectural history. The earliest remains are floor 1 and wall A, which are associated with each other. Wall B is cut into the surface of floor 1, and wall A is overlain by floor 2. Both wall A and floor 1 therefore went out of use when floor 2 and wall B were built. Subsequently the floor was renewed (floor 3) while wall B remained in use. Wall C was then built, cutting through floor 3 to rest its foundations on floor 2; but floor 3 remained in use, the foundation trench for wall C being covered over by a patch. Only later was wall B demolished and floor 3 replaced by floor 4. After K.B.

will be other evidence which was not found in the place where it originally stood. For example, on an Iron Age site in western Europe there is often plenty of burnt clay daub lying about. On a Roman site, tiles, plaster, pieces of flooring, perhaps even a fragment of stone lintel or column, will usually be scattered around and inside the building (Fig. 57). With all such evidence assembled in the form of plans, drawings and photographs, interpretation can begin. (A certain amount of interpretation in fact takes place during the excavations, but this is preliminary and subject to alteration later.)

The first stage of interpretation must be in terms of history; that is, the whole sequence of structural remains must be established and drawings made of the remains of each

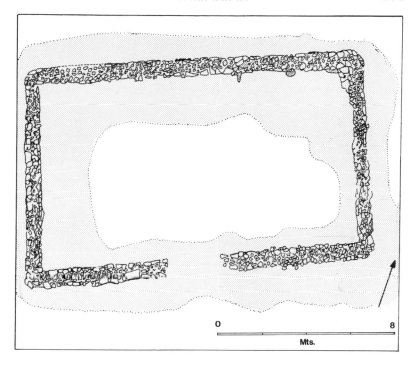

60. Plan of a farm building in the native settlement at Butcombe, Somerset, showing the extent of the rubble which had tumbled or been dislodged from the walls. The small amount of tumble suggests that these could never have been much higher than the four courses preserved at the north-east corner, and that the building was largely of timber, erected on stone footings. The structure and the enclosure in which it stands date to *c.* AD 270-350, but overlie a succession of earlier structures dating back to perhaps the fifth century BC. After P.J. Fowler

individual phase. This is essential, for the master plan will show the sum total of remains. In this respect it may be misleading, as can be seen by comparing the master plan of a small Roman villa with the excavator's interpretation of it in terms of a sequence of structures (Fig. 58). At no time were all the walls on the master plan in use together and, in this sense, it shows a non-existent building. The basis of the method by which the excavator establishes his sequence and decides which walls and floors were contemporary is stratification. In

61. An excavated tomb of *c.* 2000 BC at Kamilari in southern Crete immediately after the removal of surface soil. A mass of large stone blocks had fallen from the upper parts of the wall, the remaining section of which showed a pronounced inward lean. This was achieved by corbelling – each course of stone slightly overlapping the one below. The fallen stone and the traces of corbelling are suggestive of a circular building which may once have been covered by a complete stone vault. Photo: Doro Levi

other words, the archaeologist must sort out which floors are cut through by which walls; which floors run up to the walls and which overlie the grubbed-out foundations of other walls, and so on. Obviously this exercise is much easier when dealing with stone walls and substantial floors than with structures represented by a mass of post-holes and at best a sequence of earth floors; but the principles remain the same (Fig. 59).

Having established the sequence of structures, the archaeologist can now tackle each building individually. Since he will very rarely find more than the foundations, the first problem is the nature of the superstructure. The foundations will give him some idea as to what this will have been like. For example, post-holes or sleeper trenches – for the placing of horizontal wooden beams – clearly imply a timber framework, while massive stone foundations are unlikely to have carried a

62. The remains of a timber building (late fourth or early fifth century AD) at Latimer, Buckinghamshire. Two parallel trenches, with straight sides and flat bottoms, are visible and, along their inner sides, four or five pairs of post-holes. This arrangement implies that sleeper-beams were laid in the trenches and that wall supports stood on them. The post-holes carried roof supports curving inwards to hold up the ridge. Photo: K.B.

light timber superstructure. But what of slighter stone foundations? These could have been used as nothing more than a sill for a wooden superstructure; the building might have been half-timbered or the walls built in stone up to the eaves. Several indications can be sought to solve this problem. The amount and extent of rubble is one obvious clue (Fig. 60). Another is the discovery of wall plaster or daub carrying impressions of hurdling or wattle. Primary evidence of roofing materials often survives in the form of tiles or slates, thick lumps of plaster bearing impressions of hurdling or wooden beams, charred fragments of beams or, in the case of stone vaulting, rows of collapsed stones (Fig. 61). The shape of the roof will be suggested by the shape of the building and the position of the roof supports inside it (Fig. 62). Roofing materials will also be borne in mind, since those of lighter weight obviously allow greater spans and introduce more flexibility – in this sense – into the arrangement of the roof

63. A stage in the reconstruction of an Iron Age house, undertaken as an experiment at Butser in Hampshire. Experimental archaeology such as this allows archaeologists to become aware of the problems facing ancient man in erecting a building, and to learn what is and is not possible within the constraints of the ground plan and structural remains for which he has found evidence. Drawing: P. Christian

supports. In the final analysis, this process of reconstructing the shell of the building will prompt the archaeologist to ask himself three questions: 'What do the surviving remains suggest?', 'Is there anything missing which would survive if my hypothesis is correct?', and 'Was the method and arrangement I postulated structurally sound and technologically possible for the people who constructed the building?'

To answer this last question, and also perhaps to try and gain further insights into the problems which faced the ancient builder, the modern archaeologist may sometimes attempt to build the structure he envisages (Fig. 63). He will use the same tools and materials that he knows were available to ancient man, and in the light of his experience in building his structure he will almost certainly revise his reconstruction. 'Experimental archaeology' of this sort is applied to a wide variety of other human activities in addition to building, and it is constantly broadening our awareness both of the problems

64. Organic furnishings and furniture survive only in very exceptional circumstances, but the observant archaeologist may sometimes find clues to them in unlikely places. Here, on the bases of two prehistoric pots from southern Europe, the impressions of rush and woven matting on which the freshly made pots had been stood before firing is still to be seen. Photo: T. Corns

facing early man and also his ingenuity in solving them.

From the shell, the archaeologist moves to the fittings. Where were the doorways? Often they will be clearly marked by thresholds, sockets, surviving fragments of jambs, different spacing of the wall supports or an outside path. Even where all of these are absent, other clues can be sought. An earth, clay or even plaster floor, for example, will usually reveal much more wear near doorways than elsewhere. If living conditions were squalid and occupation debris collected on the floor, there will usually be a much thinner deposit by the doorway, since it is unlikely that anyone would block the entrance to his living room with rubbish. On the other hand, the number of householders in ancient times who tossed their rubbish just outside their open door is remarkable – and very useful, as these deposits are another indication of the vicinity of a doorway. The subdivision of the building into rooms or areas may not be as readily apparent as in a Roman villa or a Mesopotamian town house. In prehistoric timber huts, interior

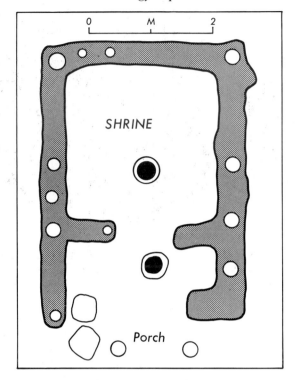

65. The ground plan of this small building inside the hillfort at South
Cadbury (Somerset) is one of several clues which cumulatively point to the
building's function. The plan is unlike that of contemporary houses standing
nearby; it also contained no domestic rubbish. It was built on the summit of
the hill in a prominent position, and the area before it was lined by a series of
pits containing animal burials. Taking all these features into consideration
the excavator reasonably suggests that the building was a shrine or temple.
After L. Alcock

partitions may have consisted of nothing more than skins hung
from rafters, leaving no visible remains, or at best thin wattle
walls which might be traceable in the form of stake-holes in
the floor. In such circumstances these partitions are suggested
by differences in the wear and nature of the floor, the
distribution of small finds and the spread of occupation debris,
as well as from more obvious features like hearths and ovens.
Although furniture rarely survives, the position of beds,

cupboards and so on can sometimes be fixed by very regularly shaped areas of floor where occupation debris and wear are absent. The use of woven mats on the floor may be betrayed by tell-tale impressions on the bases of pots (Fig. 64).

The identification of two-storey buildings is often very difficult. Except for substantial flights of stone steps, stairs seldom survive; but wooden ones can sometimes be identified where stair-wells – usually small square or oblong rooms with a strong supporting cross wall or central pier – can be recognised. More frequently, however, the only evidence for a second storey is where the debris and artifacts from the upper floor are found lying on the collapsed ceiling materials of the room below. Many of the famous Linear B tablets from the Minoan palace of Knossos were found in this situation.

Little has so far been said about identifying the function of a building; in many cases this presents little difficulty. If it is not revealed by the plan of the building and its fittings, then very often the answer can be found in the material inside and around it. The most frequent exceptions to this rule are buildings which have served a ritual function (Fig. 65). Here, the problem is not only to identify with certainty the religious nature of the building, but also to establish whether it was used privately or communally. In most ancient societies cult furniture, such as cult figures, altars, offering tables, figurines, sacrificial deposits, lamps and ritual pits, is remarkably uniform, so that many shrines can confidently be identified as such. The point at which this or any other identification of function is made will vary from site to site and structure to structure. A provisional identification of the function of a building will have been arrived at by most excavators while they are digging it, and few approach the task of interpretation without a reasonably clear idea of what they think it was used for. This may seem to be putting the cart before the horse; in fact, the function of a building will often determine not only its interior decoration and fittings but also, to varying degrees, its design and construction.

From this brief description of the way an archaeologist approaches the interpretation of structural remains, it should be possible to understand the basis of all archaeological interpretation. The secret of successful and correct deduction lies largely, but not entirely, in the collection of evidence. The more information the archaeologist can acquire from his observations in the field and in the library, and the more evidence his array of specialists can extract from the various groups of material, the better will be his chances of providing a correct and comprehensive reconstruction of his site in antiquity. Similarly, the greater his experience and knowledge of the human and natural environment of the site, the more accurate and detailed will be his reconstruction of it in all its aspects. But beyond knowledge and information lies something more – a mixture of intuition and a controlled use of the imagination. Often it is only by the combined use of all these resources that the archaeologist can answer the question 'What was it?'

10. Why is excavation so slow?

At first sight this might seem to be a thinly veiled request for a time-and-motion study of archaeologists and excavations. The comment, so often expressed by onlookers, that labourers could do it all so much more quickly carries implicit questions: 'Why is it necessary to remove the soil so carefully?', 'Why the need for expertise and skill?', and, in the final analysis, 'Why archaeologists? Cannot anyone expose walls and floors and collect coins and pottery?' The simple answer is that anyone can, but he will be left with walls, floors and pottery and little else. The amount of information he will gather will be negligible and, in the long term, so too will be the sense of satisfaction. Though the initial thrill of discovery will remain, the deeper rewards of detection and deduction, interpretation and reconstruction will be lost.

It should by now be clear why excavation must be left in the hands of skilled and trained specialists. Only by training and experience do excavators know what to look for and what is significant. Only a trained and experienced eye will recognise the importance, or even the existence, of slight changes in the colour or texture of the soil. These may represent almost anything from a scrap of rotted leather to the post-holes and sleeper-trenches of a very large building. It seems most unlikely that anyone but highly trained and experienced archaeologists would have discovered the scarcely visible traces of the great Saxon palace at Cheddar, whose presence was detected in this way (Fig. 66).

The amount of time an archaeologist spends on an excavation, however, would be much less if he were only concerned with the actual digging of the site. But he is trained not only to excavate and observe, he must also record. Excavation is by nature destructive; once a site has been excavated it is gone for good, and the work cannot be repeated. For this reason, a complete and accurate record of the archaeologist's discoveries is as important as the skilled use of the best and latest excavation and preservation techniques.

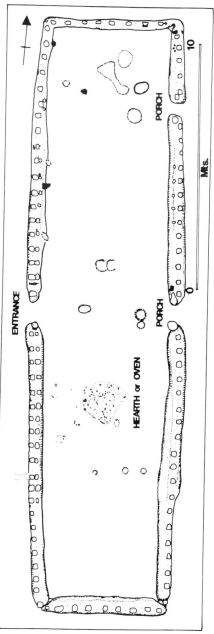

66. Diagram of a Saxon long hall at Cheddar, Somerset, of which no physical remains survived for the excavators to find. It was traced only by changes in the colour and texture of the soil at points where there had once been post-sockets and the trench in which they were placed. It had been a substantial building, about 80ft long and made entirely of timber; it is thought to date to the ninth century AD. Excavation of such sites requires not only care and expertise but a great deal of time. After P. Rahtz

67. The deep stratified deposits in the Purron Cave, Mexico, exemplify the kind of excavation work that can only be carried out by trained observers of minor differences in the colour and texture of soils. The dozens of levels, many of them floors with plant and animal remains on them, are visible in the photograph but were very difficult to recognise at the time of excavation. Each level had to be isolated and then excavated without contamination from the levels above and below, and finally measured and drawn on a detailed section. Photo: R.S. MacNeish

This will mean that during his work on a site the archaeologist will make dozens, perhaps hundreds, of plans, sections and sketches, each requiring many measurements to be made. Each post-hole, for example, is usually drawn both in plan and in profile. A single section may have several dozen individual levels in it, each of which has to be measured in at short, regular intervals (Fig. 67). In addition, both the small finds and the general finds are carefully recorded – the small finds three-dimensionally. All in all, many notebooks full of on-the-spot observations are made and hundreds of photographs taken. Recently, computerised recording of excavation data has been developed. All this requires a great deal of time, but if it is done properly the site can be reinterpreted any time in the future. In this respect the excavation reports of General Pitt-Rivers, who excavated widely on Cranborne Chase, Wiltshire, in the late nineteenth century are adjudged to be remarkable. Sixty years afterwards, Professor Hawkes was able to reinterpret the sites in such detail that it might be called a case of 're-excavation on paper'. Of course, Pitt-Rivers did not keep soil samples or mollusca, nor did he collect pollen grains; in the 1880s no one knew how much information could be obtained from such evidence. But the modern archaeologist does know, and consequently takes soil samples and collects snail shells, along with samples of charcoal and mortar and others, for archaeomagnetic or C14 dating. This not only takes time but demands considerable knowledge of what constitutes a good sample of each technique and the correct methods of individual collection and storage. This work cannot be left to the untrained excavator, who may know his prehistory and excavating techniques but will usually be unaware of the intricacies of collecting samples. Archaeology today is both too broad and too specialised to be a suitable field of activity for either the dilettante or the single-minded 'digger' bent only on 'finding things'.

Although the period of excavation may seem long to the outsider, it is but a small fraction of the total amount of time an archaeologist will spend investigating his site. As has been explained, a considerable amount of preparatory work needs to be done before he even begins excavating. A great deal more work, in terms of study, preservation and interpretation, is

68. Many man-hours were needed to excavate even this 'unassuming hollow' of a Saxon grubenhaus inside the defences of the Saxon Shore fort at Portchester, Hampshire. This small hut with sunken floor is typical of pagan Saxon settlements of the fifth century AD. Although architecturally simple, such huts may take up to fifty hours of careful work by modern excavation techniques. Further time will be required for the treatment of finds, and for recording the remains of the structure. Later come the longer processes of preserving the finds, studying and analysing material from the occupation layers and comparing it with that from other sites, and finally preparing the definitive report of the hut and its contents. Photo. B.W. Cunliffe

necessary when the excavation is over. Depending on the type of site excavated, large quantities of flint-work, pottery, animal bones and other materials will have to be washed, sorted perhaps three or four times, and then carefully studied in detail. Drawings must be made of many of these items, and for some of them the archaeologist will try to find parallels from other excavations which may throw additional light on the history or the importance of his own site. While he is thus engaged on the collections of human artifacts, other specialists will be working on the soil samples, pollen grains, animal

69. One of the more unusual parts of a modern archaeologist's career. Dr John Collis, who has excavated two prehistoric barrows in the Peak District, here dons nineteenth-century clothes and becomes the great Victorian barrow-digger, Thomas Bateman, for the sake of a young audience at a special museum event. Using the knowledge gained from his own and other recent excavations, the twentieth-century archaeologist is able to reinterpret and draw new information from those of his Victorian predecessor. Photo: T. Corns

bones, plant remains and other materials recovered. A conservationist will begin the task of permanently preserving many of the finds which had only received 'first aid' at the time of discovery. Finally, there is the writing and publishing of a definitive report on the excavation and its results. This will involve many months of careful marshalling of the evidence, and providing drawings and photographs to illustrate it. How long does all this take? Some years ago, Professor Barry Cunliffe estimated the amount of man-hours spent by himself and his colleagues on the excavation, subsequent study and interpretation of a Saxon grubenhaus, or hut, at Portchester Castle in Hampshire (Fig. 68). The grubenhaus, like others of its kind, survived as little more than 'an unassuming hollow' – a mere ten square metres of excavation. Even so, 83 hours were required for excavation and recording, and for the finds to receive preliminary treatment. With the work of study, interpretation and publication still unfinished at the time of Professor Cunliffe's estimate, another 165 hours had already been devoted to post-excavation work on the hut and its contents.

Seen in this light, and bearing in mind the amount of information which the skilled and careful archaeologist will wring from even the most unproductive sites, excavations lasting two, four or even eight or ten weeks may perhaps be regarded more favourably. For every week of excavation – and of possible inconvenience to a farmer, a contractor, a builder or to the public in general – the archaeologist will, for many more weeks, strive to extract the maximum amount of information from his evidence. In time, the outcome of his endeavours will give museum staff the opportunity to prepare new displays to feed the results back to the public (Fig. 69). Some of these displays will take the traditional form, with plans and photographs, models and objects grouped together in a series of show cases, along with explanatory labels, describing the finds and their significance. Other displays may be of a very different kind. They may involve activity sessions where children (and adults too) can try their hand at prehistoric methods of making pots, preparing and cooking food, or spinning and weaving cloth. Then again, it may be possible to reconstruct an ancient building, either in the

70. Another way in which the fruits of long and painstaking excavation, followed by further months of study and research, eventually lead to a vivid experience of the past for modern visitors. Here, on the site of a Roman fort of about AD 60, the Royal Engineers in co-operation with the archaeologists have reconstructed the gateway and rampart of the fort as we believe it would have looked. The timbers stand in their original Roman sockets, and the superstructure is based on Roman depictions of their forts. The Lunt, Baginton, near Coventry. Photo: K.B.

museum or even on the original site. At West Stow, Suffolk, it is possible to see a reconstructed Anglo-Saxon grubenhaus, which immediately gives a vivid impression of what Professor Cunliffe's 'unassuming hollow' at Portchester may once have looked like. At Bagington near Coventry it is possible to walk through the gates of a first-century Roman fort – rebuilt on the original site, but by today's army instead of the Roman one (Fig. 70). At Biskupin in Poland you can walk into the reconstructed homes of people who lived there in 600 BC. All of this is possible because of the painstaking months of excavation and research by trained and skilled archaeologists.

Some of the more outstanding discoveries may feature in

television programmes, and the new information will appear in books on the shelves of public libraries. People who visited the excavations in the field may see these displays, films and books, and to the questions they asked then – and around which this book has been written – they will begin to add others. Who were the people who lived on this site? Where did they come from? How did they live? What did they believe in? A whole new area of interest will be opened up to them, and here is an immediate justification for all those months of work. Beyond it lie those deeper motivations for archaeology which were discussed in the first chapter. Man needs a tangible past, and archaeology provides it.

Bibliography

There are many introductory books on archaeology which cover some or all of the topics introduced in this book in greater detail, and those listed below are only a selection.

P. Fowler *Approaches to Archaeology* (1977)
K. Greene *Archaeology: an Introduction* (1983)
J. Hester and J. Grady *Introduction to Archaeology* (1981)
D. Miles *An Introduction to Archaeology* (1978)
J. Smith *Foundations of Archaeology* (1976)

Books which elaborate on certain specific topics include:

Chapter 2: P. Rahtz (ed.) *Rescue Archaeology* (1974)
G. Clark *Archaeology and Society* (1964)

Chapter 4: M. Aston and T. Rowley *Landscape Archaeology* (1974)
S.S. Frere and J.K. St Joseph *Roman Britain from the Air* (1983)
L. Duel *Flights into Yesterday* (1978)

Chapter 5: J.G. Evans *An Introduction to Environmental Archaeology* (1978)

Chapter 7: C. Wells *Bones, Bodies and Disease* (1964)
K. Manchester *The Archaeology of Disease* (1984)

Chapter 8: A.C. Renfrew *Before Civilisation* (1973)

Chapter 9: J. Coles *Archaeology by Experiment* (1973)
A. Sorrell *Reconstructing the Past* (1981)

Index

Page numbers in bold type refer to illustrations.